GOD'S DESIGN
FOR CHEMISTRY

PROPERTIES
OF ATOMS &
MOLECULES

Debbie & Richard Lawrence

Answers
in Genesis®

God's Design for Chemistry is a complete chemistry curriculum for elementary aged children. The books in this series are designed for use in the Christian homeschool, and provide easy to use lessons that will encourage children to see God's hand in everything around them.

2nd Printing: March 2006

ISBN: 1-893345-83-1

Cover design: Brandie Lucas
Layout: Diane King
Editor: Gary Vaterlaus

Published by *Answers in Genesis*, PO Box 510, Hebron, Kentucky 42080

Printed in the United States of America

You may contact the authors at: info@rdeducation.com; (970) 686-5744

www.AnswersInGenesis.org

CONTENTS

Welcome to
God's Design for Chemistry

God's Design for Chemistry is a series that has been designed for use in teaching chemistry to children in grades 3-7. It is divided into two books: *Properties of Matter* and *Properties of Atoms and Molecules.* Each book has approximately 35 lessons as well as a unit project that ties all of the lessons together.

In addition to the lessons, special features in each book include biographical information on interesting people as well as interesting facts pages to make the subject more fun and a little less dusty.

Please use the books in this series as a guide and feel free to add to each lesson. Although this is a complete curriculum, the information included here is just a beginning. A resource guide is included in Appendix B to help you find additional information and resources. Also, a supply list of items needed is included at the beginning of each lesson. A master list of all supplies needed for the entire book can be found in Appendix C.

If you wish to cover the material in this series in one year you should plan on covering approximately 2 lessons per week. The time required for each lesson varies depending on how much additional information you want to include, but you can plan on about 45 minutes per lesson. Older children can do quizzes, tests or additional activities on non-lesson days if you choose to do science every day.

If you wish to cover material in more depth, you may add additional information and take a longer period of time to cover all the material.

Why Teach Chemistry?

Maybe you hate science or you just hate teaching it. Maybe you love science but don't quite know how to teach it to your children. Maybe science just doesn't seem as important as some of those other subjects you need to teach. Maybe you need a little motivation. If any of these descriptions fits you, then please consider the following.

It is not uncommon to question the need to teach your kids hands-on science in elementary school. We could argue that the knowledge gained in science will be needed later in life in order for your children to be more productive and well-rounded adults. We could argue that teaching your children science also teaches them logical and inductive thinking and reasoning skills, which are tools they will need to be more successful. We could argue that science is a necessity in this technological world in which we live. While all of these arguments are true, none of them are the main reason that we should teach our children science. The most important reason to teach science in elementary school is to give your children an understanding that God is our Creator, and the Bible can be trusted. Teaching science from a creation perspective is one of the best ways to reinforce your children's faith in God and to help them counter the evolutionary propaganda they face every day.

God is the Master Creator of everything. His handiwork is all around us. Our Great Creator put in place all of the laws of physics, biology and chemistry. These laws were put here for us to see His wisdom and power. In science, we see the hand of God at work more than in any other subject. Romans 1:20 says, "For since the creation of the world His invisible attributes are clearly seen, being understood by the things that are made, even His eternal power and Godhead, so that they [men] are without excuse." We need to help our children see God as Creator of the world around them so they will be able to recognize God and follow Him.

The study of chemistry helps us understand and appreciate the amazing way everything God created works together. The study of atoms and molecules and how different substances react with each other reveals an amazing design, even at the smallest level of life. Understanding the carbon, nitrogen and water cycles helps our children see that God has a plan to keep everything working together.

It's fun to teach chemistry! It's interesting too. The elements of chemistry are all around us. Children naturally like to combine things to see what will happen. You just need to direct their curiosity.

Finally, teaching chemistry is easy. You won't have to try to find strange materials for experiments or do dangerous things to learn about chemistry. Chemistry is as close as your kitchen or your own body.

How Do I Teach Science?

In order to teach any subject you need to understand how people learn. People learn in different ways. Most people, and children in particular, have a dominant or preferred learning style in which they absorb and retain information more easily.

If your child's dominant style is:

Auditory – he needs to not only hear the information but he needs to hear himself say it. This child needs oral presentation as well as oral drill and repetition.

Visual – he needs things he can see. This child responds well to flashcards, pictures, charts, models, etc.

Kinesthetic – he needs active participation. This child remembers best through games, hands-on activities, experiments and field trips.

Also, some people are more relational while others are more analytical. Your relational child needs to know who the people are, why this is important and how it will affect him personally. Your analytical child, however, wants just the facts.

If you are trying to teach more than one child, you will probably have to deal with more than one learning style. Therefore, you need to present your lessons in several different ways so that each child can grasp and retain the information. You need to give them a reason to learn it.

To help you with this, we have divided each lesson into three sections. The first section introduces the topic. It is the "just the facts" part of the lesson for the analytical child. This section is marked by the ✎ icon. The second section is the observation and hands-on section denoted by the 🔍 icon. This section helps your visual and kinesthetic learners. The final section is the summary and review section denoted by the 🎁 icon, representing wrapping up the lesson. This oral review helps your auditory learners. Also included in this section is the applications part of the lesson to help your relational child appreciate what he has learned. We have included periodic biographies to help your child appreciate the great men and women who have gone before us in the field of science.

We suggest a threefold approach to each lesson:

✎ INTRODUCE THE TOPIC

- We give a brief description of the facts. Frequently you will want to add more information than the bare essentials given in this book. This section of each lesson is written as if we were talking to your child. In addition to reading this section aloud, you may wish to do one or more of the following:

- Read a related book with your child.

- Write things on the board to help your visual child.

- Give some history of the subject. We provide some historical sketches to help you, but you may want to add more.

- Ask questions to get your child thinking about the subject.

🔍 MAKE OBSERVATIONS AND DO EXPERIMENTS

- One or more hands-on projects are suggested for each lesson. This section of each lesson is written to the child, but may require help from the parent/teacher.

- Have your child observe the topic for him/herself whenever possible.

🎁 WRAP IT UP

- The "What did we learn?" section has review questions.

- The "Taking it further" section encourages your child to

    o   Draw conclusions

o   Make applications of what was learned

o   Add extended information to what was covered in the lesson

The "FUN FACT" section adds fun information.

(Questions with answers are provided to help you wrap up the lesson.)

By teaching all three parts of the lesson, you will be presenting the material in a way that all learning styles can both relate to and remember.

Also, this method relates directly to the scientific method and will help your child think more scientifically. Don't panic! The "scientific method" is just a way to logically examine a subject and learn from it. Briefly, the steps of the scientific method are:

1.   Learn about a topic.

2.   Ask a question.

3.   Make a hypothesis (a good guess).

4.   Design an experiment to test your hypothesis.

5.   Observe the experiment and collect data.

6.   Draw conclusions. (Does the data support your hypothesis?)

Note: It's okay to have a "wrong hypothesis." That's how we learn. Be sure to try to understand why you got a different result than you expected.

Our lessons will help your child begin to approach problems in a logical, scientific way.

How Do I Teach Creation vs. Evolution?

We are constantly bombarded by evolutionary ideas about life, which prompt many questions. Is a living being just a collection of chemicals? Did life begin as a random combination of chemicals? Can life be recreated in a laboratory? What does the chemical evidence tell us about the earth? The Bible answers these questions and this book accepts the historical accuracy of the Bible as written. We believe this is the only way we can teach our children to trust that everything God says is true.

There are 5 common views of the origins of life and the age of the earth:

1.   Historical biblical account – Each day of creation in Genesis is a normal day of about 24 hours in length, in which God created everything that exists. The earth is only thousands of years old, as determined by the genealogies in the Bible.

2.   Progressive creation - The idea that God created various creatures to replace other creatures that died out over millions of years. Each of the days in Genesis represents a long period of time (day-age theory) and the earth is billions of years old.

3.   Gap theory – The idea that there was a long, long time between what happened in Genesis 1:1 and what happened in Genesis 1:2. During this time, the "fossil record" was supposed to have formed, and millions of years of Earth history supposedly passed.

4. Theistic evolution – The idea that God used the process of evolution over millions of years (involving struggle and death) to bring about what we see today.

5. Naturalistic evolution – The view that there is no God and evolution of all life forms happened by purely naturalistic processes over billions of years.

Any theory that tries to add the evolutionary timeframe with creation presupposes that death entered the world before Adam sinned, which contradicts what God has said in His Word. The view that the Earth (and its "fossil record") is hundreds of millions of years old damages the Gospel message. God's completed creation was "very good" at the end of the sixth day (Genesis 1:31). Death entered this perfect paradise *after* Adam disobeyed God's command. It was the punishment for Adam's sin (Genesis 2:16-17; 3:19; Romans 5:12-19).

The first animal death occurred when God killed at least one animal, shedding its blood, to make clothes for Adam and Eve (Genesis 3:21). If the Earth's "fossil record" (filled with death, disease and thorns) formed over millions of years before Adam appeared (and before he sinned), then death no longer would be the penalty for sin. Death, the "last enemy" (1 Corinthians 15:26), and diseases (such as cancer) would instead be part of the original creation that God labeled "very good." No, it is clear that the "fossil record" formed some time *after* Adam sinned—not many millions of years before. Most fossils were formed as a result of the worldwide Genesis Flood.

When viewed from a biblical perspective, the scientific evidence clearly supports a recent creation by God, and not naturalistic evolution and millions of years. The volume of evidence supporting the biblical creation account is substantial and cannot be adequately covered in this book. If you would like more information on this topic, please see the resource guide in Appendix B. To help get you started, just a few examples of evidence supporting a recent creation are given below:

• **Evolutionary Myth:** Life evolved from non-life when chemicals randomly combined together to produce amino acids and then proteins that then produced living cells. **The Truth:** The chemical requirements for DNA and proteins to line up just right to create life could not have happened through purely natural processes. The process of converting DNA information into proteins requires at least 75 different protein molecules. But each and every one of these 75 proteins must be synthesized in the first place by the process in which they themselves are involved. How could the process begin without the presence of all the necessary proteins? Could all 75 proteins have arisen by chance in just the right place at just the right time?[1] Dr. Gary Parker says this is like the chicken and the egg problem. The obvious conclusion is that both the DNA and proteins must have been functional from the beginning, otherwise life could not exist. The best explanation for the existence of these proteins and DNA is that God created them.[2]

• **Evolutionary Myth:** Stanley Miller created life in a test tube, thus demonstrating that the early earth had the conditions necessary for life to begin. **The Truth:** Although Miller was able to create amino acids from raw chemicals in his famous experiment, he did not create anything close to life or even the ingredients of life. There are four main problems with Miller's

[1] John P. Marcus, in: Ashton, J., ed., *In Six Days: Why 50 scientists choose to believe in creation*, Master Books, 2000, 177.

[2] Gary Parker, *Creation Facts of Life*, Creation Life Publishers, 1994, 24-28.

experiment. First, he left out oxygen because he knew that oxygen corrodes and destroys amino acids very quickly. However, rocks found in every layer of the earth indicate that oxygen has always been a part of the earth's atmosphere. Second, Miller included ammonia gas and methane gas. Ammonia gas would not have been present in any large quantities because it would have been dissolved in the oceans. And there is no indication in any of the rock layers that methane has ever been a part of the earth's atmosphere. Third, Miller used a spark of electricity to cause the amino acids to form, simulating lightning. However, this spark more quickly destroyed the amino acids than built them up, so to keep the amino acids from being destroyed, Miller used specially designed equipment to siphon off the amino acids before they could be destroyed. This is not what would have happened in nature. And finally, although Miller did produce amino acids, they were not the kinds of amino acids that are needed for life as we know it. Most of the acids were ones that actually break down proteins, not build them up.[3]

• **Evolutionary Myth:** Living creatures are just a collection of chemicals. **The Truth:** It is true that cells are made of specific chemicals. However, a dead animal is made of the same chemicals as it was when it was living, but it cannot become alive again. What makes the chemicals into a living creature is the result of the organization of the substances, not just the substances themselves. Dr. Parker again uses an example. An airplane is made up of millions of non-flying parts; however, it can fly because of the design and organization of those parts. Similarly, plants and animals are alive because God created the chemicals in a specific way for them to be able to live.[4] A collection of all the right parts is not life.

• **Evolutionary Myth:** Chemical evidence points to an earth that is billions of years old. **The Truth:** Much of the chemical evidence actually points to a young earth. For example, radioactive decay in the earth's crust produces helium atoms that rise to the surface and enter the atmosphere. Assuming that the rate of helium production has always been constant (an evolutionary assumption), the maximum age for the atmosphere could only be 2 million years. This is much younger than the 4+ billion years claimed by evolutionists. And there are many ideas that could explain the presence of helium that would indicate a much younger age than 2 million years.[5] Similarly, salt accumulates in the ocean over time. Evolutionists claim that life evolved in a salty ocean 3-4 billion years ago. If this were true and the salt has continued to accumulate over billions of years, the ocean would be too salty for anything to live in by now. Using the most conservative possible values (those that would give the oldest possible age for the oceans), scientists have calculated that the ocean must be less than 62 million years. That number is based on the assumption that nothing has affected the rate at which the salt is accumulating. However, the Genesis Flood would have drastically altered the amount of salt in the ocean, dissolving much sodium from land rocks.[6] Thus, the chemical evidence does not support an earth that is billions of years old.

[3]   Ken Ham, et al., *War of the Worldviews*, Master Books, 2006, 15-24. See also www.AnswersInGenesis.org/origin.
[4]   Parker, op. cit., 29-30.
[5]   See Dr. Don DeYoung, *Thousands…not billions*, Master Books, 2005. See also: www.AnswersInGenesis.org/helium.
[6]   John D. Morris, Ph.D., *The Young Earth*, Creation Life Publishers 1994, 83-87. See also www.AnswersInGenesis.org/creation/v21/i1/seas.asp

Atoms and Molecules

Elements

Bonding

Chemical Reactions

Acids and Bases

Biochemistry

Applications of Chemistry

Unit Activity & Conclusion

LESSON 1

INTRODUCTION TO CHEMISTRY

THE STUDY OF MATTER AND MOLECULES

SUPPLY LIST:

Drinking glass
Baking soda
Vinegar

Chemistry may sound like a big word and a difficult subject to study, but it's not. Chemistry is simply the study of matter and matter is anything that has mass and takes up space. Some examples of matter are water, wood, air, food, paper, your pet skunk or your little brother. So if you are interested in learning more about anything around you, then you are ready to learn about chemistry.

Chemists are scientists who study what things are made of, how they react to each other and how they react to their environment. Chemistry is the study of the basic building blocks of life and the world.

In chemistry you will learn about atoms and molecules. You will learn about how substances combine to make other substances. You will find out how a substance changes form and you will discover that God created our world with such intricate designs that we may never fully understand how everything works.

God has established laws that govern how chemicals react and how matter changes. Many of these laws seem mysterious because they happen on an atomic level. Although, these changes cannot be seen with the naked eye, the results of these laws can be seen all around us. As you study atoms and molecules you will begin to understand these laws and appreciate the beauty of God's design on the tiny level of the atom.

GOD'S DESIGN FOR CHEMISTRY
PROPERTIES OF ATOMS & MOLECULES

Atoms and Molecules

Elements

Bonding

Chemical Reactions

Acids and Bases

Biochemistry

Applications of Chemistry

Unit Activity & Conclusion

CHEMISTRY IS FUN:

As you will learn in the upcoming lessons, some materials are very stable and do not change easily. Other materials are very reactive and easily combine with other substances to make a new substance. For a fun experiment try the following:

Place 1 teaspoon of baking soda in a drinking cup. Pour 1 tablespoon of vinegar into the cup. Now watch the reaction!

Vinegar is an acid and baking soda is a base. Acids and bases easily combine together to form salts. In this reaction they also produce a gas. Can you guess what that gas might be? It is carbon dioxide.

WHAT DID WE LEARN?

What is matter? (Anything that has mass and takes up space?)

Does air have mass? (Yes. It may seem like there is nothing there, but even though air is very light, it still has mass. The air contains molecules that take up space.)

What do chemists study? (The way matter reacts with other matter and the environment.)

TAKING IT FURTHER

Would you expect to see the same reaction each time you combine baking soda and vinegar? (Yes, because God designed certain laws for matter to follow so we would expect it to react the same way each time.)

Atoms and Molecules

Elements

Bonding

Chemical Reactions

Acids and Bases

Biochemistry

Applications of Chemistry

Unit Activity & Conclusion

LESSON

2

ATOMS

BASIC BUILDING BLOCKS

SUPPLY LIST:

1 copy of "Atomic Models" worksheet per child (pg. 7)

Everything around you is made of matter. But what is matter made of? This is a question that has interested scientists for thousands of years. It is obvious that water is a different kind of substance than a rock and that a person is very different from a tree. But what makes each thing unique? As scientists considered this question, they began to try to separate and break down different substances to understand what they were made of. Eventually, scientists have discovered that everything in the universe is made of vary small particles called atoms. Atoms are the smallest part of matter that cannot be broken down by ordinary chemical means. Atoms are so small that we cannot see them, even with the best microscope. But we can see how different types of atoms behave and see how they combine with other atoms.

Because atoms are so small, scientists have had to develop models to describe what an atom is like. Have you every played with a toy truck or airplane? That toy was a model of the real thing. It allowed you to see the basic parts of the vehicle, but it was not the same size or as complex as the real thing. In the same way, models of atoms help us to understand the basic parts of an atom, but they are not the same size or as complex as a real atom.

The earliest written ideas showing that matter was made of atoms come from the Greeks around 400 BC. The Greek scientists believed that matter was made of very small particles. But they did not try to describe those particles. Work on an actual atomic model did not really begin until the 1700s when experimental science became more popular. Early experiments showed that different atoms had different masses. In 1897, it was discovered that atoms consisted of electrically charged particles and that some particles in the atom were smaller than others. By 1911, a scientist

GOD'S DESIGN FOR CHEMISTRY
PROPERTIES OF ATOMS & MOLECULES

Atoms and Molecules

Elements

Bonding

Chemical Reactions

Acids and Bases

Biochemistry

Applications of Chemistry

Unit Activity & Conclusion

named Rutherford discovered that atoms consisted of a positively charged nucleus with negatively charged particles whirling around it. And finally, Neils Bohr discovered that the electrons whirling around the nucleus had different energy levels.

All of these discoveries have helped in the development of the current atomic model. Today scientists describe an atom as having three parts: protons, neutrons and electrons. Protons are positively charged particles. Neutrons are neutral; they do not have a positive or negative charge. And electrons are negatively charged particles. All of the parts of an atom are extremely small; however, electrons are much smaller than protons and neutrons. Protons and neutrons are approximately 1800 times more massive than electrons.

The protons and neutrons in an atom are combined together in a tight mass called the nucleus. The electrons circle around the nucleus like the moon orbiting the earth. However, the electrons orbit so quickly that it is not possible to say exactly where a particular electron is at any given moment. Also, some electrons orbit more closely to the nucleus than others. It is believed that the electrons in an atom occupy different levels, or distances, from the nucleus depending on how much energy they have.

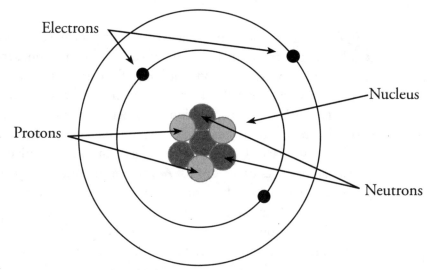

The model of a lithium atom above shows its nucleus containing four neutrons and three protons. It also shows three electrons orbiting the nucleus. Two electrons orbit closer to the nucleus, and the third electron orbits further away.

In all atoms, the lowest energy level, that which is closest to the nucleus, is filled with electrons first. If a level is full, electrons will occupy the next level. The first level can hold up to two electrons. If an atom has more than two electrons, two electrons will orbit close to the nucleus, and the others will begin to fill the next layer. The chart on the next page shows how many electrons scientists believe that each energy level can hold. Note however that the highest number of electrons that has been determined to be in any energy level is 32 because an inner energy level does not have to be full

GOD'S DESIGN FOR CHEMISTRY
PROPERTIES OF ATOMS & MOLECULES

Atoms and Molecules

Elements

Bonding

Chemical Reactions

Acids and Bases

Biochemistry

Applications of Chemistry

Unit Activity & Conclusion

before the next level begins to fill up. For example, even though the fourth level can hold 32 electrons, the fifth level begins filling up after the fourth level has only 8 electrons in it.

CHART OF MAXIMUM ELECTRONS IN EACH ENERGY LEVEL

Energy Level	Maximum Number of Electrons
1	2
2	8
3	18
4	32
5	50
6	72
7	98

The electrons orbiting in the energy level furthest from the nucleus of an atom are called valence electrons. The lithium model shows that lithium has one valence electron. Valence electrons play a vital role in how an element behaves. Neutral atoms are ones in which the number of electrons equals the number of protons. However, atoms can gain or lose valence electrons. If an atom has a number of electrons different from the number of protons in the nucleus, it is called an ion and it has an electrical charge. If the ion has more electrons than protons, it has a negative charge. If it has fewer electrons than protons, it has a positive charge. The ability to gain, lose or share valence electrons is what allows different atoms to bond with each other to form new molecules.

The number of protons in the nucleus of an atom determines what kind of atom it is. If an atom loses or gains a neutron, or loses or gains an electron, it is still the same type of atom. But if the atom loses or gains a proton, it becomes a different type of material. Regardless of the number of neutrons or electrons that an atom may have, a lithium atom always has three protons.

As research into the structure of atoms continues, scientists continue to gain more understanding of the complexity of the atom. It is believed that protons, neutrons and electrons are made of smaller particles called quarks, but because of their extremely small size, they are difficult to study. This complexity continues to amaze scientists and shows God's mighty hand in the design of the universe.

ATOMIC MODELS:

Color the parts of the atoms on the "Atomic Models" worksheet.

WHAT DID WE LEARN?

What is an atom? (The smallest part of matter that cannot be broken

GOD'S DESIGN FOR CHEMISTRY
PROPERTIES OF ATOMS & MOLECULES

Atoms and
Molecules

Elements

Bonding

Chemical
Reactions

Acids and Bases

Biochemistry

Applications of
Chemistry

Unit Activity
& Conclusion

down by ordinary chemical means.)

What are the three parts of an atom? (Protons, neutrons and electrons)

What electrical charge does each part of the atom have? (Protons are positive, neutrons are neutral and electrons are negative.)

What is the nucleus of an atom? (The dense center of the atom consisting of protons and neutrons)

What part of the atom determines what type of atom it is? (The number of protons in the nucleus determines what kind of atom it is.)

What is a valence electron? (An electron in the outermost energy level for that atom)

TAKING IT FURTHER

Why is it necessary to use a model to show what an atom is like? (Atoms are too small to see and are very complex, so a model is useful for understanding what an atom is like.)

On your worksheet, you colored neutrons blue and protons green. Are neutrons actually blue and protons actually green in a real atom? (No, the colors used in a model are just to help us visualize the parts. They do not really represent the actual colors.)

FUN FACT

The models used to represent atoms do not accurately show the size relationship between the nucleus and the electrons. If the nucleus of the atom was the size of a tennis ball, the electrons would be orbiting about 1 mile away.

ATOMIC MODELS

Color the protons in each atom green, the neutrons blue and the electrons orange.

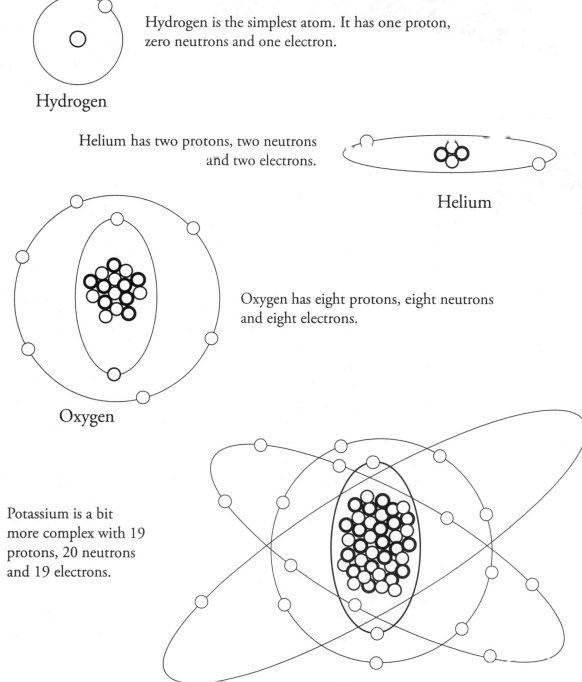

Hydrogen is the simplest atom. It has one proton, zero neutrons and one electron.

Hydrogen

Helium has two protons, two neutrons and two electrons.

Helium

Oxygen has eight protons, eight neutrons and eight electrons.

Oxygen

Potassium is a bit more complex with 19 protons, 20 neutrons and 19 electrons.

Potassium

Atoms and Molecules

Elements

Bonding

Chemical Reactions

Acids and Bases

Biochemistry

Applications of Chemistry

Unit Activity & Conclusion

ATOMIC MASS

HOW BIG IS AN ATOM?

SUPPLY LIST:

1 copy of "Understanding Atoms" worksheet per child (pg. 11)

As you learned in the previous lesson, an atom consists of three parts: protons, neutrons and electrons. You also learned that the number of protons determines the type of element the atom will be. Therefore, the number of protons in an atom is called the atomic number. Hydrogen, which only has one proton, has an atomic number of 1. Oxygen, which has eight protons in its nucleus, has an atomic number of 8. The atomic number of an atom is very useful in identifying the type of atom.

The mass of an atom is also an important characteristic to know about the atom. The mass of an atom is determined by the number of protons and neutrons in the atom. Electrons are so small and contribute such a tiny amount to the mass that their mass is considered insignificant. The mass number or atomic mass of an element is found by adding the number of protons and the number of neutrons in the atom. For example, hydrogen has only one proton and no neutrons so its atomic mass is one. Oxygen, which has eight protons and eight neutrons, has an atomic mass of 16.

Because the mass of a proton or neutron is so small, it would not make sense to measure an atom's mass in grams. So a special unit has been defined for measuring the mass of an atom. This unit is an atomic mass unit, or amu (it is also called *unified atomic mass unit*, and abbreviated as u). An amu is defined as 1/12 the mass of a carbon atom. A carbon atom has six protons and six neutrons, and thus has an atomic mass of 12 amu. Protons and neutrons have nearly identical masses, so for most applications an amu can be used to describe the mass of either type of particle. The mass of an

GOD'S DESIGN FOR CHEMISTRY
PROPERTIES OF ATOMS & MOLECULES

Atoms and
Molecules

Elements

Bonding

Chemical
Reactions

Acids and Bases

Biochemistry

Applications of
Chemistry

Unit Activity
& Conclusion

electron is 1800 times smaller than that of a proton or neutron, so we usually say its mass is negligible—it can be ignored.

If you look at the atomic mass for most elements, you find that most are not listed as whole numbers. This does not mean that an atom has only part of a proton or part of a neutron. It means that even though all atoms of a particular element have the same number of protons, some have different numbers of neutrons. Each variety of atom is called an isotope of that element. To help you understand this better, let's look at carbon. On most periodic tables, the atomic mass of carbon is listed as 12.01 amu. This is an average of carbon atoms that naturally occur. All carbon atoms have 6 protons or they would not be carbon atoms. And most of the time carbon atoms have 6 neutrons giving them an atomic mass of 12. However, some carbon atoms, a very small percentage, have extra neutrons in their nuclei. This isotope of carbon usually has two extra neutrons so these atoms have an atomic mass of 14 amu. (Isotopes are forms of an element that have different numbers of neutrons in their nucleus, and thus different atomic masses.) When you average the mass of all carbon atoms, the average comes out to 12.01. Some isotopes of other elements have additional neutrons and some have fewer neutrons than the majority of the atoms that occur. Therefore, the average mass for most atoms is not a whole number.

LEARNING ABOUT ATOMS:

Complete the "Understanding Atoms" worksheet.

WHAT DID WE LEARN?

What are the three particles that make up an atom? (Proton, electron and neutron)

What is the atomic number of an atom? (The number of protons in the nucleus)

What is the atomic mass of an atom? (The average sum of the protons and neutrons in the nucleus of the atom)

How can you determine the number of electrons, protons and neutrons in an atom if you are given the atomic number and atomic mass? (The number of protons is the same as the atomic number. The number of electrons is equal to the number of protons. The number of neutrons is equal to the atomic mass minus the number of protons. To find the most common number of neutrons, round the atomic mass to the nearest whole number before subtracting the number of protons.)

TAKING IT FURTHER

What does a hydrogen atom become if it loses its electron? (A proton)

Why are atomic masses usually not whole numbers? (Sometimes an atom has an extra neutron or has fewer neutrons than the majority of that type of atom. This is called an isotope. The atomic mass is an average of a random sample of naturally occurring atoms.)

Why are electrons ignored when calculating an element's mass? (The mass of an electron is so small compared to the mass of a proton or neutron that it does not make a significant difference.)

UNDERSTANDING ATOMS

Use the Periodic Table of the Elements on page 21 to help fill in the chart below. The symbol for each element is in bold letters near the top of each square. The atomic number (which is equal to the number of protons) is above the symbol. The atomic mass is below the symbol.

Element Name	Symbol	Atomic Number	Atomic Mass	Number of Protons	Number of Electrons	Most Common Number of Neutrons
Hydrogen						
Oxygen						
Boron						
Gold						
Silver						
Uranium						
Potassium						
Chlorine						
Neon						
Einsteinium						

MADAME CURIE

(1867-1934)

Atoms, isotopes and radioactive decay are the things that Marie Curie is best known for. But who was she? When she was born in 1867, her last name was Sklodowska. She was born in Warsaw, Poland, an area that was controlled by the czar of Russia at that time. Because of their pro-Polish leanings, Marie's parents lost their jobs and her father was forced into a series of lower academic posts. The family was poor and took in students as boarders to help pay the rent. When Marie was eight, her oldest sister died, and less than three years later her mother also died. This made the family turn to each other for strength.

As they were growing up, their father read them classics and exposed them to science. Marie graduated from high school at the age of 15, at the top of her class. But, women were not allowed to attend the University of Warsaw, so Marie went to a floating university, named so because it changed locations frequently to hide it from the Russian authorities. This schooling was not a high quality education, so Marie made a pact with her older sister. Marie would work and help send her sister to Paris for medical school, then her sister would work to send her to school. For two years, Marie worked as a teacher and then, to make more money, she became a governess and sent as much money as she could to her sister.

Eventually, Marie went back home and because of her father's new job she was able to leave for Paris in 1891, when she was 24 years old. There, life was hard for her. In the winters, she would wear every piece of clothing she had to keep herself warm. And sometimes she would get so absorbed in her studies she would forget to eat and she would pass out. In later years, Marie said it was very common for the Polish students to be poor.

When she arrived in Paris, Marie found that she was ill prepared for college. She was lacking in both math and science, plus her technical French was behind where it needed to be. She overcame this by working hard and it paid off. She graduated first in her class for her Master's degree in physics and second in her class in math the following year.

n 1894, Marie began sharing lab space with a man named Pierre Curie. Their work drew them together, and in July 1895, the two were married in a simple ceremony. In September of

1897, their first child was born, a baby girl. Pierre's father delivered the baby. A few weeks later Pierre's mother died and Pierre's father, along with Marie, Pierre and baby Irene moved into a house together. Marie kept working in the lab and found her father-in-law to be the prefect babysitter.

About six months after Marie and Pierre were married, a German physicist named Henri Becquerel discovered a ray produced by uranium that could travel through wood and flesh and produce an image on photographic paper. Because the ray was an unknown type of ray, he named it X-ray. He won the first Nobel Prize for Physics for this discovery.

Marie and Pierre soon started working with uranium. They discovered other materials that also emitted strong rays and they called this characteristic radioactivity. One of the most important radioactive materials discovered by the Curies was radium. It wasn't long before radium was in demand. In cheap novels, it was touted as "a magical substance whose rays could cure all ills, power wondrous machines or destroy a city at one blow." This obviously was quite an exaggeration; however, the damaging effects radioactivity has on tissues was soon used on cancer cells. These damaging effects also took their toll on both Marie and her husband. Pierre developed sores on his body and was constantly fatigued. Marie lost 20 pounds and her fingertips were scarred from the radiation, but they had no knowledge of the long-term effects. While they noted Pierre's loss of good health and the severe pains he experienced, they did not link this to their work.

In 1903, both Pierre and Marie were invited to England to be honored for their work at the Royal Institution. Because it was not customary for women to speak there, Lord Kelvin showed his support for Marie by sitting next to her as her husband gave his speech. Later, when Pierre was nominated for the Nobel Prize in Physics for his and Marie's discovery of radium, he said it would be a travesty if his wife was not also included; so she was. In 1911, Marie received a second Nobel Prize, this one in chemistry, for the discovery of the atomic mass of radium.

After Pierre was killed by a horse-drawn wagon in 1906, Marie continued to carry on their work. A little while later, she was offered and accepted her husband's academic post at the Sorbonne, becoming the first woman to teach at this prestigious French college. Over the next few years with the help of some wealthy friends and the French government, she was able to found the Radium Institution where research into the uses of radium in treating cancer and other illnesses was to be conducted.

When war came to France in 1914, the Radium Institute was complete, but Marie had not moved in yet. The other researchers who worked there were drafted to fight the Germans, and Marie also wanted to help. She knew X-rays could help save soldiers' lives by showing the doctors where the bullets or shrapnel were located, and they could see how the bones were broken. So she helped design 20 radiology vans to be taken into the field to treat the wounded. Since no one else was trained to use the X-ray equipment, Marie learned how to drive and she and her very mature 17 year old daughter, along with a doctor, made the first trip to the front lines in the fall of 1914. By 1916, Marie was training other women to work in the 20 mobile units and at the 200 stationary units.

After the war, Marie went back to work at the Radium Institute, and between 1919 and her death from leukemia in 1934, the Institute published 483 works, including 31 papers and books by Marie. Both of her daughters also achieved distinction. Irene and her husband won a Nobel Prize, and her daughter Eve was recognized for her writings. But the Curies will continue to be best known for their discovery of radioactivity.

Atoms and
Molecules

Elements

Bonding

Chemical
Reactions

Acids and Bases

Biochemistry

Applications of
Chemistry

Unit Activity
& Conclusion

MOLECULES

PUTTING ATOMS TOGETHER

LESSON 4

SUPPLY LIST:

1 copy of "Molecule Puzzle Pieces" per child (pg. 16)

Atoms seldom exist by themselves. Instead, most atoms bond with other atoms. A group of chemically connected atoms is called a molecule. How atoms will connect with each other is determined by the number of valence electrons each atom has. If the outermost layer of electrons is full, the atom will be stable and unlikely to bond with other atoms; however, there are only six elements that are stable by themselves. All other atoms will combine with other atoms to create a full outer layer of electrons.

Some atoms combine with other atoms of the same element. For example, oxygen atoms are seldom found by themselves. Instead, two oxygen atoms usually combine together. When two atoms of the same material combine to form a molecule the result is called a diatomic (meaning two atoms) molecule. Oxygen is the most common diatomic molecule, but several other gases exist as diatomic molecules as well, including hydrogen, nitrogen and fluorine.

When atoms of different elements combine together to form a molecule, it is called a compound. The most common compound on earth is water, which is a combination of two hydrogen atoms and one oxygen atom. God has created the elements in such a way that multiple atoms can combine together in nearly innumerable ways. So far, over three million compounds have been identified.

When atoms combine to form compounds, the new substance that is formed has completely different characteristics from the elements that form it. For example, sugar is formed from carbon, hydrogen and oxygen atoms. Yet the sweet compound we use in so many baked goods has no resemblance to carbon—which is best known as coal—or hydrogen or

GOD'S DESIGN FOR CHEMISTRY
PROPERTIES OF ATOMS & MOLECULES

Atoms and Molecules

Elements

Bonding

Chemical Reactions

Acids and Bases

Biochemistry

Applications of Chemistry

Unit Activity & Conclusion

oxygen, which are both colorless gases.

We will explore how and why atoms bond together in more detail in later lessons. For now, just know that atoms connect together because of the number of valence electrons they have. And remember that the new materials formed by these combined atoms are very different from the elements that produce them.

MAKING MOLECULES:

Cut out each piece of the "Molecule Puzzle Pieces" worksheet. Now try to figure out which elements will combine together to form rectangles. The shape of each element piece represents the number of valence electrons it has. Molecules will be stable if they have eight valence electrons. Hydrogen and helium are the only elements that are stable with only two electrons in their outer energy level.

Try the following combinations:

- Two hydrogen pieces together—this forms the diatomic molecule H2

- Two hydrogen pieces and one oxygen piece—this forms a water molecule

- One sodium and one chlorine—this forms table salt

- Neon cannot combine with any of the other pieces because it already has a full set of eight electrons in its outer level.

WHAT DID WE LEARN?

What is a molecule? (Two or more atoms chemically connected or bonded together)

What is a diatomic molecule? (A molecule with two of the same type of atoms connected together)

What is a compound? (A molecule made from two or more different kinds of atoms)

TAKING IT FURTHER

What is the most important factor in determining if two atoms will bond with each other? (The number of valence electrons each atom has.)

Table salt is a compound formed from sodium and chlorine. Would you expect sodium atoms and chlorine atoms to taste salty? Why or why not? (No, because when molecules are formed, the resulting compound is a new substance with its own characteristics, completely different from those of the original elements.)

MOLECULE PUZZLE PIECES

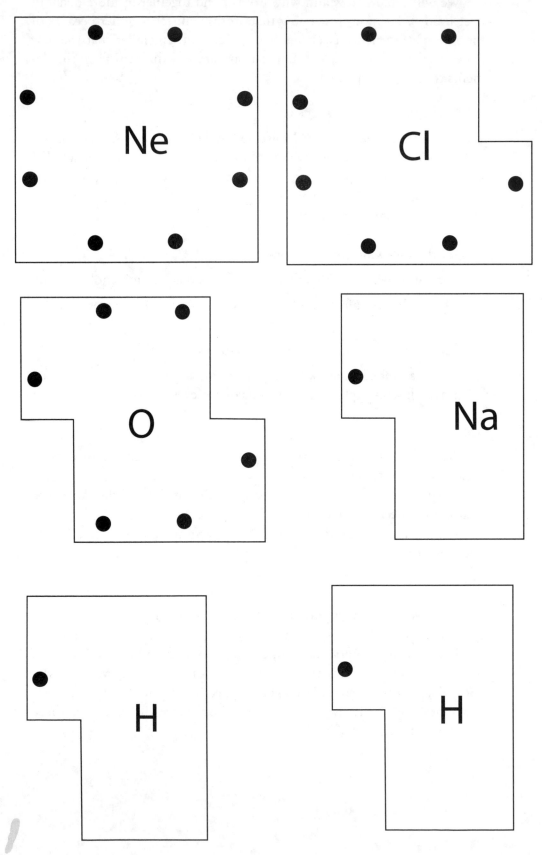

Atoms and Molecules Quiz

Lessons 1-4

Label the parts of this helium atom.

A. _____

B. _____

C. _____

B and C together form the _____

Matching:

1. Anything that has mass and takes up space   valence electrons

2. A positively charged particle in an atom   neutron

3. A negatively charged particle in an atom   molecule

4. A neutral particle in the nucleus   matter

5. The outermost electrons   proton

6. Compact center of the atom   atom

7. Two atoms of the same element connected together   diatomic molecule

8. Part of matter that cannot be broken down chemically   atomic number

9. Number of protons an element has   electron

10. Two or more atoms chemically bonded   nucleus

Complete the following chart—Refer to the Periodic Table of the Elements on page 21:

Element	Atomic #	Atomic Mass	# of protons	# of electrons	# of neutrons
Carbon					
Aluminum					
Tungsten					

(Note: answers to all quizzes and tests are in Appendix A)

Atoms and Molecules

Elements

Bonding

Chemical Reactions

Acids and Bases

Biochemistry

Applications of Chemistry

Unit Activity & Conclusion

LESSON 5

THE PERIODIC TABLE OF THE ELEMENTS

ORGANIZING THE ELEMENTS

SUPPLY LIST:

1 copy of "The Periodic Table of the Elements" for each child (pg. 21)
Crayons, markers or colored pencils

Keeping track of information for all of the elements that have been discovered can be a big task. Fortunately for you, much of that information can be found in a Periodic Table of the Elements. Periodic tables sometimes have additional information, but all periodic tables have at least the following information. Each square will show the name of the element, the symbol for the element, the atomic number and the atomic mass. Remember that the atomic number is equal to the number of protons in the nucleus and the atomic mass is the average of the number of protons plus neutrons in naturally occurring isotopes of that particular element. The symbol is 1, 2 or 3 letters derived from the name of the element.

The elements in the table are arranged in columns, called families, by the number of valence electrons each atom has. The number of valence electrons affects how the element reacts with other elements, so grouping elements together this way allows us to see which elements are likely to react in similar ways. Each column has a label that consists of a Roman numeral and either the letter A or B. The first column is column IA and is the family of elements called the alkali metals. Because these elements have only one valence electron, they are highly reactive.

Column IIA, the second column, consists of elements that have two valence electrons. This family is called the alkali-earth metals. These elements are also highly reactive. The middle columns, labeled IB – VIIIB, are called the transition elements. These metals all have either one or two

GOD'S DESIGN FOR CHEMISTRY
PROPERTIES OF ATOMS & MOLECULES

Atoms and
Molecules

Elements

Bonding

Chemical
Reactions

Acids and Bases

Biochemistry

Applications of
Chemistry

Unit Activity
& Conclusion

valence electrons and are often used to make metal alloys. Column IIIA is the boron family. These elements all have three valence electrons.

Column IVA is the carbon family. All elements in this family have four valence electrons. Column VA is the nitrogen family with five valence electrons, and column VIA is the oxygen family with six valence electrons. Column VIIA is called the halogen family. With seven valence electrons, these elements are highly reactive. And the final column, VIIIA, is the family called the noble gases. These elements have eight valence electrons and are very stable. The noble gases do not easily react with any other element; they are sometimes called inert gases.

The elements in the table are arranged in rows by the number of energy levels that contain electrons. Hydrogen and Helium are the only elements in the first row because the first energy level can only hold two electrons. The second row has eight elements because the second energy level can hold up to eight electrons. Even though the third energy level can hold up to 18 electrons, there are only eight elements in row 3. This is because the fourth energy level begins filling before the third level is full. Therefore, the lower energy levels may not be completely full in elements in the 3rd through 7th rows. To make this easier to understand, the periodic table on page 21 includes the number of electrons in each energy level for each element.

It should be noted that the elements above 105 have been discovered or developed in just the past few years. Most of these elements are very unstable and their characteristics are relatively unknown. At this time, elements 117 and 118 are still hypothetical.

ALL IN THE FAMILY:

Using the copy of the "Periodic Table of the Elements," review the following information:

- The top number in each box is the atomic number = the number of protons
- The bold letters are the symbol = an abbreviation for the element name
- The number below the symbol is the atomic mass = average number of protons + neutrons
- Below the atomic mass is the name of the element
- Below the name is the electron configuration

Now color the columns of the table to indicate each family as follows:

Column IA – alkali metals – red
Column IIA – alkali-earth metals – orange
Columns IB-VIIIB – transition metals – yellow

> Note that the two rows of boxes at the bottom are part of rows 6 and 7 and belong to the transition metals.

GOD'S DESIGN FOR CHEMISTRY
PROPERTIES OF ATOMS & MOLECULES

Atoms and Molecules

Elements

Bonding

Chemical Reactions

Acids and Bases

Biochemistry

Applications of Chemistry

Unit Activity & Conclusion

Column IIIA – boron family – light green
Column IVA – carbon family – dark green
Column VA – nitrogen family – light blue
Column VIA – oxygen family – dark blue
Column VIIA – halogens – pink
Column VIIIA – noble gases – purple

WHAT DID WE LEARN?

How many valence electrons do the elements in each column have? (See chart pg. 21)

What four pieces of information are included for each element in any Periodic Table of the Elements? (The element name, symbol, atomic number and atomic mass)

What do all elements in a column on the periodic table have in common? (They have the same number of valence electrons.)

What do all elements in a row on the periodic table have in common? (They have electrons in the same number of energy levels.)

TAKING IT FURTHER

Atoms are stable when they have eight electrons in their outermost energy level. Therefore elements from column IA will react easily with elements from which column? (Column VIIA)

Elements from column IIA will react easily with elements from which column? (Column VIA)

FUN FACT

When lighter-than-air ships were first designed, many were filled with hydrogen. Hydrogen is the lightest known element, thus making the ships float easily. However, after a terrible fire in the Hindenberg airship in 1937, it was decided that hydrogen was too dangerous. It was believed at the time that since hydrogen has only one electron and is highly reactive, that the fire was caused by lightning, or some other spark, causing the hydrogen to react with oxygen leading to the terrible tragedy. After this tragic accident, it was decided to change from hydrogen to helium. Helium is a noble gas. It is very stable and does not react easily with other elements, yet it is still much lighter than air and allows blimps to be used in many areas still today.

Later researchers believe that the fire in the Hindenberg was not a result of the hydrogen gas. It is now believed that the aluminum powder varnish used to coat the outside of the ship built up a huge electrostatic charge and caught fire when the electricity was discharged. They believe this fire would have started regardless of the gas used inside the ship.

THE PERIODIC TABLE OF ELEMENTS

Legend:
- Atomic number 12
- Symbol .... **MG**
- Atomic Mass 24.31
- Name .... Magnesium
- Electron structure by energy level 2,8,2

IA	IIA	IIIB	IVB	VB	VIB	VIIB	VIIIB	VIIIB	VIIIB	IB	IIB	IIIA	IVA	VA	VIA	VIIA	VIIIA
1 **H** 1.008 Hydrogen 1																	2 **He** 4.0026 Helium 2
3 **Li** 6.941 Lithium 2,1	4 **Be** 9.012 Beryllium 2,2											5 **B** 10.81 Boron 2,3	6 **C** 12.01 Carbon 2,4	7 **N** 14.01 Nitrogen 2,5	8 **O** 16 Oxygen 2,6	9 **F** 19 Fluorine 2,7	10 **Ne** 20.18 Neon 2,8
11 **Na** 22.99 Sodium 2,8,1	12 **Mg** 24.31 Magnesium 2,8,2											13 **Al** 26.98 Aluminum 2,8,3	14 **Si** 28.09 Silicon 2,8,4	15 **P** 30.97 Phosphorus 2,8,5	16 **S** 32.07 Sulfur 2,8,6	17 **Cl** 35.45 Chlorine 2,8,7	18 **Ar** 39.95 Argon 2,8,8
19 **K** 39.1 Potassium 2,8,8,1	20 **Ca** 40.08 Calcium 2,8,8,2	21 **Sc** 44.96 Scandium 2,8,9,2	22 **Ti** 47.9 Titanium 2,8,10,2	23 **V** 50.94 Vanadium 2,8,11,2	24 **Cr** 52 Chromium 2,8,13,1	25 **Mn** 54.94 Manganese 2,8,13,2	26 **Fe** 55.85 Iron 2,8,14,2	27 **Co** 58.93 Cobalt 2,8,15,2	28 **Ni** 58.69 Nickel 2,8,16,2	29 **Cu** 63.55 Copper 2,8,18,1	30 **Zn** 65.39 Zinc 2,8,18,2	31 **Ga** 69.72 Gallium 2,8,18,3	32 **Ge** 72.59 Germanium 2,8,18,4	33 **As** 74.92 Arsenic 2,8,18,5	34 **Se** 78.96 Selenium 2,8,18,6	35 **Br** 79.9 Bromine 2,8,18,7	36 **Kr** 83.8 Krypton 2,8,18,8
37 **Rb** 85.47 Rubidium 2,8,18,8,1	38 **Sr** 87.62 Strontium 2,8,18,8,2	39 **Y** 88.91 Yttrium 2,8,18,9,2	40 **Zr** 91.22 Zirconium 2,8,18,10,2	41 **Nb** 92.91 Niobium 2,8,18,12,1	42 **Mo** 95.94 Molybdenum 2,8,18,13,1	43 **Tc** -99 Technetium 2,8,18,14,1	44 **Ru** 101.1 Ruthenium 2,8,18,15,1	45 **Rh** 102.9 Rhodium 2,8,18,16,1	46 **Pd** 106.4 Palladium 2,8,18,17,1	47 **Ag** 107.9 Silver 2,8,18,18,1	48 **Cd** 112.4 Cadmium 2,8,18,18,2	49 **In** 114.8 Indium 2,8,18,18,3	50 **Sn** 118.7 Tin 2,8,18,18,4	51 **Sb** 121.8 Antimony 2,8,18,18,5	52 **Te** 127.6 Tellurium 2,8,18,18,6	53 **I** 126.9 Iodine 2,8,18,18,7	54 **Xe** 131.3 Xenon 2,8,18,18,8
55 **Cs** 132.9 Cesium -18,18,8,1	56 **Ba** 137.3 Barium -,18,18,8,2	57 **La** 138.9 Lanthanum -18,18,9,2	72 **Hf** 178.5 Hafnium -18,32,10,2	73 **Ta** 180.9 Tantalum -18,32,11,2	74 **W** 183.9 Tungsten -18,32,12,2	75 **Re** 186.2 Rhenium -18,32,13,2	76 **Os** 190.2 Osmium -18,32,14,2	77 **Ir** 192.2 Iridium -18,32,15,2	78 **Pt** 195.1 Platinum -18,32,17,1	79 **Au** 197 Gold -18,32,18,1	80 **Hg** 200.5 Mercury -18,32,18,2	81 **Tl** 204.4 Thallium -18,32,18,3	82 **Pb** 207.2 Lead 18,32,18,4	83 **Bi** 209 Bismuth -18,32,18,5	84 **Po** (209) Polonium -18,32,18,6	85 **At** (210) Astatine -18,32,18,7	86 **Rn** (222) Radon -18,32,18,8
87 **Fr** (223) Francium -18,32,18,1	88 **Ra** (226) Radium -18,32,18,8,2	89 **Ac** (227) Actinium -18,32,18,9,2	104 **Rf** (261) Rutherfordium	105 **Db** (262) Dubnium	106 **Sg** 262.94 Seaborgium	107 **Bh** (264) Bohrium	108 **Hs** (265) Hassium	109 **Mt** (266) Meitnerium	110 **Ds** (271) Darmstadtium	111 **Rg** (280) Roentgenium	112 **Uub** (285) Ununbium	113 **Uut** (284) Ununtrium	114 **Uuq** (289) Ununquadium	114 **Uup** (288) Ununpentium	116 **Uuh** (292) Ununhexium	117 **Uus** (?) Ununseptium	118 **Uuo** (?) Ununoctium

Lanthanides:

58 **Ce** 140.1 Cerium -18,20,8,2	59 **Pr** 140.9 Praseodymium -18,21,8,2	60 **Nd** 144.2 Neodymium -18,22,8,2	61 **Pm** (145) Promethium -18,23,8,2	62 **Sm** 150.4 Samarium -18,24,8,2	63 **Eu** 152 Europium -18,25,8,2	64 **Gd** 157.3 Gadolinium -18,25,9,2	65 **Tb** 158.9 Terbium -18,27,8,2	66 **Dy** 162.5 Dysprosium -18,28,8,2	67 **Ho** 64.9 Holmium -18,29,8,2	68 **Er** 167.3 Erbium -18,30,8,2	69 **Tm** 168.9 Thulium -18,31,8,2	70 **Yb** 173 Ytterbium -18,32,8,2	71 **Lu** 175 Lutetium -18,32,9,2

Actinides:

90 **Th** 232 Thorium -18,32,18,10,2	91 **Pa** 233 Protactinium -18,32,20,9,2	92 **U** 238 Uranium -18,32,21,9,2	93 **Np** (237) Neptunium -18,32,22,9,2	94 **Pu** (244) Plutonium -18,32,24,8,2	95 **Am** (243) Americium -18,32,25,8,2	96 **Cm** (247) Curium -18,32,25,9,2	97 **Bk** (247) Berkelium -18,32,26,9,2	98 **Cf** (251) Californium -18,32,28,8,2	99 **Es** (252) Einsteinium -18,32,29,8,2	100 **Fm** (257) Fermium -18,32,30,8,2	101 **Md** (258) Mendelevium -18,32,31,8,2	102 **No** (259) Nobelium -18,32,32,8,2	103 **Lr** (262) Lawrencium -18,32,32,9,2

DEVELOPMENT OF THE PERIODIC TABLE

The Periodic Table of the Elements, which is probably the most important tool a chemist has, is a table that lists some of the most important properties known about each element. But like all tools, someone had to invent it. So how did this useful tool come into existence?

In the early 1800s many scientists tried to find relationships between the various elements, but this was a daunting task, somewhat like sorting the pieces of a jigsaw puzzle without knowing what the picture should be. In 1866, an English scientist named John Newlands began sorting the then-known elements according to their atomic masses. He believed that the properties of the elements repeated every eighth element and he called this the law of octaves. However, there were many elements that did not fit into this pattern and eventually it was discarded. Only three years later, in 1869, a Russian chemist named Dmitri Mendeleev came up with what is considered by most people to be the first periodic table of elements.

Dmitri Mendeleev was born in Siberia, Russia, in 1834, and was the youngest of at least 14 children. About the time Dmitri finished high school, his father died and his mother moved to St. Petersburg, Russia, where she worked hard to earn the money needed to send Dmitri to college. This sacrifice paid off, not only for Dmitri, but also for all scientists to follow.

After college, Mendeleev began to catalog all the data he could find on the 63 elements known at the time. He was sure that the elements had repeating or "periodic" properties. He wrote the properties of each element on a card, and then he arranged the cards according to their similar properties and in order of their increasing atomic masses. Mendeleev found that this method worked very well for most elements, and for the few that did not fit, he did a very unusual thing; he moved the element over one space and left a hole. He was convinced that where holes appeared, elements would be found in the future to fill these holes. He was so sure of this that he even predicted what the properties of the elements would be. And over the next several years, these predicted elements were indeed discovered.

The shape of the table has changed several times as scientists have discovered new elements, but the concept developed by Mendeleev has remained the same. The biggest advance to the periodic table after Mendeleev was in 1914, when Henry Moseley decided to arrange the elements according to their atomic numbers instead of their atomic masses. This arrangement solved some of the problems in Mendeleev's table and led to the periodic table we use today.

Atoms and Molecules

Elements

Bonding

Chemical Reactions

Acids and Bases

Biochemistry

Applications of Chemistry

Unit Activity & Conclusion

LESSON 6

METALS

SILVER AND GOLD HAVE I NONE...

SUPPLY LIST:

Flashlight with battery
Copper wire

Electrical or duct tape

What do you think of when you hear that something is made of metal? Do you think of something hard, heavy, strong and shiny? That would be a pretty good description of most metals. Do you think of cars, washing machines, silverware or coins? Those are just a few of the many uses for metal.

Three quarters of all elements on earth are metals. Most are hard, strong and heavy. However, a few pure metals are weak or soft. The majority of metals have the following six characteristics:

1. Silvery luster on the surface

2. Solid at room temperature (except for mercury, which is a liquid)

3. Malleable – can be hammered into shape

4. Ductile – can be drawn into a wire

5. Good conductor of electricity

6. Tend to be very reactive

Most metals have 1 to 3 valence electrons. They easily give up their electrons, which is why they are reactive with many other elements. This is also why metals are good conductors of electricity. Because of their unique characteristics, metals are used in a variety of ways. Their strength and malleability allow them to be used for making cars and trucks, bridges, appliances, aluminum siding and soda pop cans. Metal's conductivity of electricity is why metal is used for electrical wiring in nearly every house and building in America.

GOD'S DESIGN FOR CHEMISTRY
PROPERTIES OF ATOMS & MOLECULES

Atoms and
Molecules

Elements

Bonding

Chemical
Reactions

Acids and Bases

Biochemistry

Applications of
Chemistry

Unit Activity
& Conclusion

As you go across the periodic table from left to right, the elements become less metallic; this means that they are less malleable, less ductile and less conductive. The dividing line between the metals and the non-metals is the diagonal line of elements that are shaded on the periodic table on page 21. These eight elements are called metalloids. They act partially like metals and partially like non-metals. The metalloids are called semi-conductors because they conduct only a small amount of electricity. This is an important characteristic for the technological world. Semi-conductors are used to provide low power yet high-speed electronic devices used in many products such as computers, digital watches and cell phones.

CONDUCTING ELECTRICITY:

One of the most important characteristics of metals is the fact that they conduct electricity. You can demonstrate this trait by doing the following

1. Cut two 12-inch pieces of copper wire. Strip about 1 inch of plastic off of each end of the wires.

2. Remove the light bulb and battery from a flashlight.

3. Using electrical tape or duct tape, tape one end of a wire to the negative terminal of the battery and the other end of the wire to the side of the metal contact on the light bulb.

4. Tape one end of the second wire to the positive terminal of the battery.

5. Touch the other end of the second wire to the end of the light bulb and watch the bulb light up.

Electrons are flowing from the battery, through the first wire, through the light bulb, through the second wire, and finally back to the battery. Because copper conducts electricity so well, it is used for most electrical wiring in buildings.

GOD'S DESIGN FOR CHEMISTRY
PROPERTIES OF ATOMS & MOLECULES

Atoms and Molecules

Elements

Bonding

Chemical Reactions

Acids and Bases

Biochemistry

Applications of Chemistry

Unit Activity & Conclusion

WHAT DID WE LEARN?

What are the six characteristics of most metals? (Silvery luster, solid, malleable, ductile, conducts electricity, reacts with other elements)

How many valence electrons do most metals have? (Most commonly, metals have 1 or 2 valence electrons, but some have 3 or 4.)

What is a metalloid? (An element that has some metal characteristics and some non-metal characteristics)

TAKING IT FURTHER

What are the most likely elements to be used in making computer chips? (The semi-conductors—the ones shaded on the Periodic Table of the Elements. The most commonly used elements are silicon, germanium and boron.)

Is Arsenic likely to be used as electrical wire in a house? (No, it is only a semi-conductor so it would not make good electrical wiring.)

FUN FACT

Manganese is the only metal that is not silvery, ductile or malleable, which may make is seem like a non-metal. However, manganese acts like a metal when it is alloyed, or added to other metals.

Atoms and
Molecules

Elements

Bonding

Chemical
Reactions

Acids and Bases

Biochemistry

Applications of
Chemistry

Unit Activity
& Conclusion

NON-METALS

THE REST OF THE ELEMENTS

SUPPLY LIST:

Drawing paper   Markers

The vast majority of the elements on earth are metals or metalloids. There are only 17 elements that are non-metals. These include hydrogen, plus the 16 elements to the right of the metalloids. Although hydrogen is listed in the left column of the periodic table because it has only one valence electron, it often acts more like the elements in column VIIA because it only needs one electron to have a full outer shell.

Non-metals have very different characteristics from metals. They generally do not have a silvery luster or shiny appearance. Because the non-metals need only one to three electrons to fill their outer shells, they do not easily give up electrons, but share or gain electrons when they combine with other elements. Because they do not give up electrons, non-metals are poor conductors of electricity. At room temperature, some non-metals are solid, some are liquid but most are gases. Those that are solid are usually brittle and shatter easily.

The top four elements in column VIIA are called halogens. These are very reactive elements. These elements can be very dangerous in large quantities, but in small quantities they are very useful. Chlorine is added to drinking water and swimming pools to kill bacteria. Fluorine is added to drinking water and toothpaste to prevent tooth decay. Iodine can also be used to kill germs, and is an essential nutrient in our diets. Because hydrogen is so reactive, it is sometimes grouped with the halogens.

The elements in column VIIIA are called the noble gases because they do not easily combine with any other element. Because these elements have eight electrons in their outer shells, they are very stable. They are referred to as inert gases because they do not react. Their inability to react makes

GOD'S DESIGN FOR CHEMISTRY
PROPERTIES OF ATOMS & MOLECULES

Atoms and Molecules

Elements

Bonding

Chemical Reactions

Acids and Bases

Biochemistry

Applications of Chemistry

Unit Activity & Conclusion

noble gases very useful for certain applications. Noble gases are sometimes used to fill a space instead of air to prevent a reaction from occurring. For example, in the process of making semi-conductor chips, the space around the circuitry may be filled with argon gas instead of air to prevent a reaction from occurring.

DESIGNING A NEON SIGN:

Noble gases do not easily react with other elements. However, they have another special characteristic that makes them very useful. When a noble gas is in an enclosed container and an electrical current is passed through it, the gas turns into a plasma and a colored light is given off. You have probably seen this phenomenon many times without realizing it. Most of the lighted signs that look like glass tubes that have been formed into the shape of words or symbols, like the sign on the previous page, are referred to as neon signs. When these tubes are filled with neon gas, the electrical current produces a red/orange colored glow. Not all lighted signs are neon signs. Other noble gases will produce different colors of light. This same trait of inert gases is used in plasma ball toys and plasma TV screens.

Design your own neon sign. Draw the outline of a tube that is shaped like what you would like your sign to look like. Then color it red or orange to show that it is filled with neon gas.

WHAT DID WE LEARN?

What are some common characteristics of non-metals? (Not shiny or silver, not conductive, do not easily lose electrons.)

What is the most common state for non-metal elements? (Gas)

Why are halogens very reactive? (They need only one electron to fill their outer shells.)

Why are noble gases very non-reactive? (They have a full outer shells of electrons.)

TAKING IT FURTHER

Hydrogen often acts like a halogen. How might it act differently from a halogen? (Because hydrogen has only one electron, it can give up its electron and become an ion, whereas halogens do not easily give up electrons.)

Why are balloons filled with helium instead of hydrogen? (Helium is a noble gas and non-reactive, but hydrogen is highly reactive.)

Atoms and
Molecules

Elements

Bonding

Chemical
Reactions

Acids and Bases

Biochemistry

Applications of
Chemistry

Unit Activity
& Conclusion

LESSON

8

HYDROGEN

VERY REACTIVE

SUPPLY LIST:

Vegetable oil   Margarine
Peanut butter

It's the first element listed in the periodic table and it's the smallest and simplest atom. What is it? It's hydrogen. Hydrogen has an atomic number of 1 because it has one proton and zero neutrons in its nucleus and one electron in orbit around the nucleus. This is the simplest possible atom. Hydrogen needs only two electrons to make it stable, and since it already has one, it needs only one more. Therefore, hydrogen is often classified as a halogen, because it reacts like a halogen. However, hydrogen can also give up one electron, so it sometimes acts like an alkali metal.

Hydrogen is the lightest element in the universe. If you had a swimming pool full of hydrogen, all the molecules together would only weigh about two pounds. Hydrogen has no smell, taste or color. At normal room temperature and pressure, hydrogen is a gas. Hydrogen's boiling point is -423.17 °F (-252.87 °C) and its freezing point is -434.45 °F (-259.14 °C).

Hydrogen is the most abundant element in the universe. Hydrogen is believed to be the main element comprising the sun, as well as Jupiter and Saturn. Nearly 90% of all atoms in the universe are believed to be hydrogen atoms. Yet on earth, hydrogen is only the tenth most abundant element. God made the earth different from other planets, with additional elements necessary for life to be more abundant than hydrogen.

Most of the hydrogen on earth does not exist as hydrogen gas. Most of the hydrogen is combined with other elements to form compounds. The most common compound containing hydrogen is water. Hydrogen is also found in sugars, amino acids, proteins, cellulose and fossil fuels such as oil and gasoline. And hydrogen can combine with nitrogen to form ammonia.

GOD'S DESIGN FOR CHEMISTRY
PROPERTIES OF ATOMS & MOLECULES

Atoms and Molecules

Elements

Bonding

Chemical Reactions

Acids and Bases

Biochemistry

Applications of Chemistry

Unit Activity & Conclusion

Because hydrogen is so reactive it has many uses. It combines explosively to form water, H_2O. This makes liquid hydrogen and liquid oxygen ideal as rocket fuel. Hydrogen is also being explored as an alternative form of energy for cars. Some hybrid cars now have engines that can use either compressed hydrogen or gasoline to power them.

Hydrogen is used in many chemical processes as well. Hydrogen can be used to remove oxygen from metal oxide ores in a process called reduction. A process called hydrogenation forces hydrogen molecules through a substance to change its molecular structure. For example, vegetable oil is hydrogenated to become margarine and crude oil is hydrogenated to produce gasoline. Dehydrogenation is the process that removes hydrogen atoms from a substance.

HYDROGENATION:

Hydrogenation is a process where hydrogen is added to vegetable oil at high temperature, forcing the hydrogen to bond with the oil molecules. This process causes the oil to become thicker. This allows vegetable oil to become margarine. When peanut butter is hydrogenated the peanut oil stays mixed into the peanut butter. Hydrogenated or partially hydrogenated foods are very common.

Read the list of ingredients for vegetable oil, margarine and peanut butter. Next, compare the thickness of each of these substances. How does the thickness of the margarine and the peanut butter compare to that of the oil? Which products are hydrogenated?

Look at other food labels for hydrogenated oils. You may be surprised at how many products have these substances. Possible places to look include crackers, cookies and other snack foods, cup of noodle soups and many pre-packaged meals.

WHAT DID WE LEARN?

What is the atomic structure of hydrogen? (It has one proton and one electron.)

What is the atomic number for hydrogen? (1)

What is the most common element in the universe? (Hydrogen)

Why is hydrogen sometimes grouped with the alkali metals? (It has only one electron so it often behaves like an alkali metal.)

Why is hydrogen sometimes grouped with the halogens? (It is stable if it gains one electron so it often behaves like a halogen.)

TAKING IT FURTHER

Why is hydrogen one of the most reactive elements? (Most elements must either gain electrons or lose electrons to combine with other elements. But hydrogen can do either one so it combines easily with many other elements.)

Margarine contains only partially hydrogenated oil. What do you sup-

GOD'S DESIGN FOR CHEMISTRY
PROPERTIES OF ATOMS & MOLECULES

Atoms and Molecules

Elements

Bonding

Chemical Reactions

Acids and Bases

Biochemistry

Applications of Chemistry

Unit Activity & Conclusion

pose fully hydrogenated oils are like? (They are much harder or more solid than margarine and are not easily spread.)

FUN FACT

About 1 out of every 6,000 hydrogen atoms has a neutron in its nucleus.

FUN FACT

Some scientists are beginning to test whether partially hydrogenated oils are healthy for humans. Some people believe that the molecules formed by partial hydrogenation, which are not naturally occurring, are difficult for your body to use and can actually be harmful over long periods of time.

CARBON

GRAPHITE, COAL, AND DIAMONDS

SUPPLY LIST:

Drawing paper and colored pencils   Ceramic plate
Candle   Matches

Carbon is one of the most important and interesting elements on earth. It can exist as a soft slippery powder called graphite. It can also be found in the form of a diamond, which is the hardest substance on earth. How can the same atoms form such very different substances? It depends on how the atoms are arranged. The carbon atoms in graphite line up in long chains that easily slip over each other. But the carbon atoms in diamond are arranged in a lattice network or crystalline structure that holds each atom tightly in place. How the carbon atoms line up is greatly affected by temperature and pressure.

The atomic number of carbon is 6. Carbon has six protons and usually has six neutrons in its nucleus. It also has six electrons. Two electrons are in the inner shell and four electrons are in the outer shell. Since elements are most stable when they have eight electrons in their outer shell, carbon needs to either lose four or gain four electrons. This is not easy, so instead, carbon shares its electrons with other elements to form what are called covalent bonds. In this way, carbon will combine with many other elements to form many different compounds.

Carbon is one of the most important elements in all living things. Therefore, carbon compounds are called organic compounds. All plant and animal cells are made from organic compounds. Because carbon is essential to all living things, God has designed a way for carbon to be recycled in what is called the carbon cycle. First, plants absorb carbon in the form of carbon dioxide gas from the air. This carbon dioxide is used in the photosynthesis process to form sugar. Next, animals eat the plants containing sugar and

GOD'S DESIGN FOR CHEMISTRY
PROPERTIES OF ATOMS & MOLECULES

Atoms and Molecules

Elements

Bonding

Chemical Reactions

Acids and Bases

Biochemistry

Applications of Chemistry

Unit Activity & Conclusion

absorb the carbon through digestion. Much of the carbon is released back into the atmosphere through respiration when the animal breathes, exhaling carbon dioxide. Some carbon remains in the animal's body. When the animal dies, its body decays and the carbon enters the soil. Finally, bacteria and fungi in the soil absorb the carbon from the soil, convert it into carbon dioxide, and release it into the air to begin the cycle again.

Many plants are not eaten by animals, but this does not mean that the carbon in those plants is lost. When a plant dies, it decays and the carbon enters the soil. Again, bacteria and fungi absorb the carbon and release it into the air as carbon dioxide. Also, some plants that have been buried under a large amount of mud or rock and have experienced great pressure have turned into coal. When coal is mined and then burned, it releases carbon dioxide back into the air to be used by plants again. So you can see that God designed a wonderful way to allow carbon atoms to be used over and over again to sustain life on earth.

DRAWING THE CARBON CYCLE:

Draw a picture demonstrating the carbon cycle. Be sure to include plants performing photosynthesis, animals eating plants and exhaling carbon dioxide, and animals and plants decaying. You may also want to include coal being formed in the earth and/or being mined and burned to return carbon to the air. Finally, draw arrows showing which direction the carbon is moving.

EXAMINING CARBON:

You can examine carbon by collecting a sample. Hold a ceramic plate about 5 inches above a burning candle. Slowly lower the plate until a black film forms on the bottom of the plate. This film is composed of carbon atoms. You can scrape the carbon from the bottom of the plate and feel it. You can also use the carbon to write/smear a message on a piece of paper. Answer the following questions: How does the carbon look? How does the carbon feel? Do you think these carbon atoms are more like graphite or diamond? (These carbon atoms are like graphite because they smoothly move over one another.)

WHAT DID WE LEARN?

What is the atomic number and atomic structure of carbon? (Carbon is element number 6. It has 6 protons, 6 neutrons and 6 electrons.)

What makes a compound an organic compound? (It contains carbon atoms.)

Name at least two common forms of carbon? (Graphite, coal and diamond)

What is one byproduct of burning coal? (Carbon dioxide)

GOD'S DESIGN FOR CHEMISTRY
PROPERTIES OF ATOMS & MOLECULES

Atoms and
Molecules

Elements

Bonding

Chemical
Reactions

Acids and Bases

Biochemistry

Applications of
Chemistry

Unit Activity
& Conclusion

TAKING IT FURTHER

How does the carbon cycle demonstrate God's care for His creation? (It allows carbon to be recycled and keeps life continuing on earth.)

What is the most likely event that caused coal formation? (The Genesis Flood would have buried large amounts of plants under tons of mud and water. This is the most likely cause of the large amounts of coal found in the earth.)

What would happen if bacteria and fungi did not convert carbon into carbon dioxide gas? (The carbon from dead plants and animals would become trapped in the soil and would not be able to be reused in the growth of new plants.)

Atoms and Molecules

Elements

Bonding

Chemical Reactions

Acids and Bases

Biochemistry

Applications of Chemistry

Unit Activity & Conclusion

LESSON

10

OXYGEN

A VERY ESSENTIAL ELEMENT

SUPPLY LIST:

Candle
Matches
Glass cup

Small piece of dry ice
Gloves

The most abundant element on earth is oxygen. Oxygen is also believed to be the fourth most abundant element in the universe. Oxygen is element number 8 on the Periodic Table of the Elements. It has 8 protons and usually has 8 neutrons in its nucleus. Oxygen is in column VIA because it has 6 valence electrons. This means that oxygen needs two electrons added to its outer shell to be stable.

Most often oxygen atoms are found in the atmosphere as O_2, where two oxygen atoms have bonded together to form what is called a diatomic molecule. These two atoms share electrons so they are said to have covalent bonds. A small percentage of oxygen atoms combine in groups of three atoms, O_3, also known as ozone. Most of the ozone is high in the atmosphere and protects the earth from harmful radiation coming from the sun. The fact that oxygen near the surface of the earth is O_2 and not O_3 shows God's provision for life; the type of oxygen necessary for breathing is near the surface where people and the animals are, and the type of oxygen that would be poisonous is high in the atmosphere where it can help shield the earth without harming the animals.

Oxygen is also abundant on earth in the form of water. Every water molecule has an oxygen atom in it. So between water and air, oxygen is perhaps the most critical element for life. Oxygen is also found combined with many other elements to form oxides, which are generally rocks. For

GOD'S DESIGN FOR CHEMISTRY
PROPERTIES OF ATOMS & MOLECULES

Atoms and Molecules

Elements

Bonding

Chemical Reactions

Acids and Bases

Biochemistry

Applications of Chemistry

Unit Activity & Conclusion

example, oxygen combines with silicon to form silicon oxide, which is better known as quartz.

Another vital function of oxygen is in the releasing of energy. Oxygen is necessary for most burning processes. This may not seem very vital for life, however, just as oxygen is necessary to keep a wood fire burning, oxygen is also necessary to "burn" the food you eat. Oxygen is a key element in the process of converting food into energy. This is why animals need to continually breathe oxygen.

Earth is the only planet in our solar system with an abundant supply of oxygen both in the atmosphere and in the form of water. God designed our planet to be the perfect place for life to exist.

OXYGEN—NEEDED FOR BURNING:

Oxygen is a necessary element in the combustion process. Whether you are burning wood for a campfire, a candle for a birthday cake or the food you eat for energy, oxygen is necessary. To demonstrate this, light a small candle. Cover the candle completely with a glass cup. After a few seconds the candle will go out. Why? The flame has used up the oxygen in the air and if no new air can reach the flame the burning will stop.

You can demonstrate this in another fun way. Use gloves to place a small piece of dry ice in an open container. Remove the glass and relight the candle. Now scoop a cup of gas from the container with the dry ice in it and pour the gas above the lighted candle. What happened to the candle? It went out. Why? Dry ice is frozen carbon dioxide so the gas in the container is carbon dioxide gas. Carbon dioxide gas is heavier than air so when you pour it over the candle it pushes the air molecules out of the way; it moves the oxygen away from the flame and the flame dies. So you can see that oxygen in the air is a very important element.

WHAT DID WE LEARN?

What is the atomic structure of oxygen? (Oxygen has 8 protons and 8 neutrons in the nucleus, and 8 electrons. It has 6 valence electrons.)

What is a diatomic molecule? (A molecule formed by two atoms of the same element)

How is ozone different from the oxygen we breathe? (Ozone is a molecule of three oxygen atoms. The oxygen we breathe is a molecule of two oxygen atoms. O_3 is poisonous and O_2 is not.)

GOD'S DESIGN FOR CHEMISTRY
PROPERTIES OF ATOMS & MOLECULES

Atoms and Molecules

Elements

Bonding

Chemical Reactions

Acids and Bases

Biochemistry

Applications of Chemistry

Unit Activity & Conclusion

TAKING IT FURTHER

Why does the existence of ozone in the upper atmosphere show God's provision for life on earth? (If ozone were in the lower atmosphere, it would poison all living things. But in the upper atmosphere, it protects the earth from harmful radiation.)

How do animals in the ocean get the needed oxygen to "burn" the food they eat? (Most aquatic animals have gills that extract oxygen from the water. A few, like whales and dolphins, have to surface and breathe air.)

Why are oxygen atoms nearly always combined with other atoms? (They have only six valence electrons, so they are not stable by themselves.)

ELEMENTS QUIZ

LESSONS 5-10

Short answer:

1. What do elements in a column of the periodic table have in common?

   _____

2. What do elements in a row of the periodic table have in common?

   _____

3. Which column of elements is most stable? _____

4. Elements in which column are most likely to react with elements in column VIA? _____

5. Elements in which column are most likely to react with elements in column VIIA? _____

Write metal, metalloid or non-metal to match the type of element to its characteristics:

6. _____ Silvery luster   11. _____ Not shiny

7. _____ Ductile   12. _____ Somewhat malleable

8. _____ Conducts electricity   13. _____ Most often a gas

9. _____ Does not conduct electricity 14. _____ Semi-conductor

10. _____ Solid at room temperature 15. _____ Malleable

Mark each statement as True or False:

16. _____ Hydrogen is very reactive.

17. _____ Oxygen is lighter than hydrogen.

18. _____ Hydrogen is sometimes grouped with alkali metals.

19. _____ Hydrogen is sometimes grouped with halogens.

20. _____ Hydrogen is the most common element on earth.

21. _____ All elements are recycled—they are not destroyed.

22. _____ Carbon is an organic compound.

Atoms and
Molecules

Elements

Bonding

Chemical
Reactions

Acids and Bases

Biochemistry

Applications of
Chemistry

Unit Activity
& Conclusion

IONIC BONDING

GIVING UP ELECTRONS

LESSON
11

SUPPLY LIST:

Colored mini-marshmallows   Toothpicks
Glue

Atoms chemically connect with other atoms based on the number of valence electrons each atom has. Remember that valence electrons are the electrons in the outermost energy level of the atom. Scientists have determined that each atom is mot stable when its outermost level is filled with eight electrons. The only exceptions to this are hydrogen and helium, which only have two electrons in their outermost level.

Atoms with 1 or 2 valence electrons easily give up those electrons when they bond with other atoms, allowing the next level in to become the outermost level, so that their outermost level will be full. These atoms are said to have a low electronegativity, meaning they do not hold tightly to their electrons. Atoms with 6 or 7 valence electrons easily pull electrons away from other atoms when they bond. These atoms are said to have high electronegativity; they hold tightly to their electrons.

When electrons are transferred as atoms bond, the bond that is formed is called an ionic bond. One of the most common substances that is formed by ionic bonding is table salt—sodium chloride. Sodium is in the alkali metal family and has one valence electron. Chlorine is in the halogen family and has seven valence electrons. In order to be stable, sodium must lose its one valence electron and chlorine must gain one electron. When sodium and chlorine atoms combine, the chlorine pulls one electron away from the sodium.

The chlorine atom now has one more electron than protons so it has a negative charge. It is now a negative ion. The sodium atom now has one less electron than protons so it is a positively charged ion. These two atoms stay

Atoms and
Molecules

Elements

Bonding

Chemical
Reactions

Acids and Bases

Biochemistry

Applications of
Chemistry

Unit Activity
& Conclusion

bonded together by their opposite charges and now form the compound sodium chloride—table salt. Salt crystals are formed when the positively charged sodium side of a salt molecule lines up with the negatively charged chlorine side of another salt molecule. These opposite charges hold the molecules together. Salt molecules line up to form crystal lattices as shown in the picture below.

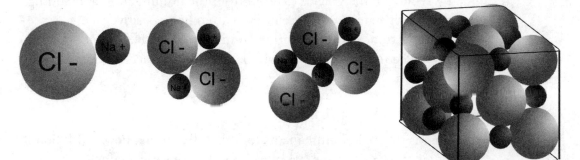

All ionic compounds, those formed by exchanging electrons, have similar characteristics.

First, ionic compounds are formed from elements that have very different electronegatvities. One element always has a high electronegativity, the other has a low electronegativity. Ionic compounds are also brittle and have high melting points. Because they are only held together by their opposite charges, ionic compounds are easily dissolved in water. The oxygen side of a water molecule is slightly negative and the hydrogen side is slightly positive; therefore, water easily pulls ionic molecules away from each other, allowing them to dissolve. Ionic compounds also conduct electricity easily when they are melted or dissolved in water.

Molecules that are formed when an atom gives up one or more electrons to another atom are called ionic compounds and their bonds are called ionic bonds because these molecules are made of ions.

ATOMIC MODELS:

Make a model of a lithium atom and a model of a fluorine atom. To make each model, use different colored mini-marshmallows for each part of the atom. If you have these colors, use green marshmallows to represent protons, yellow to represent neutrons and orange to represent electrons. Lithium has three protons and four neutrons in its nucleus. So glue together three green and four yellow marshmallows. After these have dried, break a toothpick in half and put an electron (orange marshmallow) on the end of each half. Insert these toothpicks into the nucleus. Place an electron on the end of an unbroken toothpick and insert it in the nucleus as well. This is a model of a lithium atom. Notice how two of the electrons orbit closely to the nucleus and one electron is in the outer shell.

Repeat the process to make a fluorine atom. Fluorine has 9 protons and 10 neutrons in its nucleus, so glue together 9 green and 10 yellow

GOD'S DESIGN FOR CHEMISTRY
PROPERTIES OF ATOMS & MOLECULES

Atoms and Molecules

Elements

Bonding

Chemical Reactions

Acids and Bases

Biochemistry

Applications of Chemistry

Unit Activity & Conclusion

marshmallows. The marshmallows for the nucleus can be stacked together to form a ball. After the glue has dried, again break a toothpick in half and use these short pieces to add two electrons to the atom. Finally, add 7 full-length toothpicks with electrons to the nucleus. You now have an atom that has 9 electrons, with 7 of those electrons in the outer shell.

Now demonstrate how a lithium atom and a fluorine atom would combine by removing the valence electron from the lithium atom and adding it to the fluorine atom. Now the lithium atom has a positive charge, since it lost an electron, and the fluorine atom has a negative charge, since it gained an electron. These atoms will be attracted to each other and form an ionic bond.

WHAT DID WE LEARN?

What is the main feature in an atom that determines how it will bond with other atoms? (The number of valence electrons it contains)

What kind of bond is formed when one atom gives up electrons and the other atom takes the electrons from it? (An ionic bond)

What is electronegativity? (A measure of how tightly an element holds on to its valence electrons.)

Why are compounds that are formed when one element takes electrons from another called ionic compounds? (Because ions are formed when electrons are taken away or added.)

What are some common characteristics of ionic compounds? (Conduct electricity when melted or dissolved, high melting point, soluble in water, brittle, form ions, form crystal lattices)

TAKING IT FURTHER

Which column of elements are the atoms in column IA most likely to form ionic bonds with? (The elements in column VIIA)

Which element has a higher electronegativity, chlorine or potassium? (Electronegativity increases as you go from left to right across the periodic table. Chlorine holds on to its electrons more tightly than potassium, so it has a higher electronegativity.)

Use the Periodic Table of the Elements to determine the number of electrons that barium would give up in an ionic bond. (Barium has 2 valence electrons that it would give up.)

Atoms and Molecules

Elements

Bonding

Chemical Reactions

Acids and Bases

Biochemistry

Applications of Chemistry

Unit Activity & Conclusion

COVALENT BONDING

SHARING ELECTRONS

SUPPLY LIST:

Colored mini-marshmallows   Toothpicks
Glue

Elements that give up electrons when they bond with other elements form ionic bonds. Ionic bonds occur between elements with very different numbers of valence electrons, however not all compounds are formed by ionic bonding. Sometimes atoms have a similar number of valence electrons and do not easily give them up. In this case, the elements share electrons when they bond. This type of bonding is called covalent bonding.

Compounds made by covalent bonding have very different characteristics from those formed by ionic bonding. Covalent compounds have low melting points. They are usually strong and flexible. They are also lightweight and do not easily dissolve in water. Because covalent compounds do not form ions, they do not conduct electricity very well. Also, because covalent compounds do not form ions, these molecules have only a slight attraction for each other compared to ionic compounds.

One common type of compound formed by covalent bonding is a diatomic molecule. For example, oxygen gas almost always occurs as O_2— two of the same type of atom bonded together. Each atom of oxygen has 6 valence electrons. None of these atoms will easily give up their electrons. However, when two oxygen atoms bond, they each share two of the other atom's electrons, thus making each atom seem to have a full 8 electrons in its outer shell. This allows the O_2 molecule to be stable because each atom is stable.

GOD'S DESIGN FOR CHEMISTRY
PROPERTIES OF ATOMS & MOLECULES

Atoms and Molecules

Elements

Bonding

Chemical Reactions

Acids and Bases

Biochemistry

Applications of Chemistry

Unit Activity & Conclusion

Covalent bonding does not just occur between two identical atoms. Bonds between non-metals are often covalent. The most common covalent compound on earth is water. Hydrogen has one valence electron and oxygen has six. You might think that the oxygen would pull the electron away from each of the hydrogen atoms to form ionic bonds. However, hydrogen only needs one electron to have a full outer shell so it does not easily give up its electron. Therefore, two hydrogen atoms share their electrons with one oxygen atom and the oxygen shares one of its electrons with each of the hydrogen atoms to from a water molecule. In this way, each atom feels like it has a full outer shell, so the compound is stable.

Covalent compounds are vital to life. Not only is water a covalent compound, but most of the compounds that make up our bodies are covalent compounds. These include proteins, fats and carbohydrates.

More Atomic Models:

To demonstrate covalent bonding, make marshmallow models for one oxygen and two hydrogen atoms. Use the same color of marshmallows as you did in lesson 11. Hydrogen atoms are extremely easy to make because they have only one proton and one electron. An oxygen atom has 8 protons and 8 neutrons in its nucleus and 8 electrons orbiting the nucleus. Be sure to break a toothpick in half and use the two shorter pieces for the first two electrons, thus showing that the 6 remaining electrons are in the outer shell.

Once the models are complete, set the hydrogen atoms close to the oxygen atom in such a way that the electrons of all three atoms from a group of 8 electrons in the outer layer around the nucleus of the oxygen atom. This demonstrates a covalent bond. Do not remove any electrons from any of the atoms.

What did we learn?

What is a covalent bond? (A bond formed when electrons are shared between two or more atoms.)

What are some common characteristics of covalent compounds? (Do not conduct electricity, low melting point, strong, flexible, light weight, insoluble in water, only slight attraction for each other)

What is the most common covalent compound on earth? (Water)

TAKING IT FURTHER

Why do diatomic molecules form covalent bonds instead of ionic bonds? (Diatomic molecules are formed from two atoms of the same element, so they have the same electronegativity. Since neither atom is able to take away or give up its electrons, they cannot form ionic bonds.)

Would you expect more compounds to form ionic bonds or covalent bonds? (Since there are so many metals and only a few metalloids and nonmetals, you might expect most compounds to be ionic. However, ionic bonds can be formed only by elements with very different numbers of valence electrons, thus covalent bonds are actually more common.)

Atoms and Molecules

Elements

Bonding

Chemical Reactions

Acids and Bases

Biochemistry

Applications of Chemistry

Unit Activity & Conclusion

Atoms and Molecules

Elements

Bonding

Chemical Reactions

Acids and Bases

Biochemistry

Applications of Chemistry

Unit Activity & Conclusion

METALLIC BONDING

SHARING ON A LARGE SCALE

LESSON 13

SUPPLY LIST:

Colored mini-marshmallows   Toothpicks
Glue

It is easy to see how metals and non-metals such as sodium and chlorine exchange electrons to form ionic bonds. Sodium gives up one electron so its outermost shell has 8 electrons and chlorine accepts one electron to make 8 electrons in its outermost shell. It is also easy to understand how non-metals can form covalent bonds by sharing electrons. Two oxygen atoms can share two electrons so that each atom feels that it has 8 electrons in its outer shell. However, it is more difficult to understand how metals can bond with each other. For example, aluminum, with three valence electrons, cannot form ionic bonds with other aluminum atoms. If one aluminum atom gave up its three valence electrons, the other atom would then have six valence electrons and would not be stable. If one atom gave up its three valence electrons to two other atoms there would still not be enough electrons to make the atoms stable. So you can see that metals do not form ionic bonds with other metals.

Similarly, metals do not form covalent bonds. Since metals usually have only one, two or three valence electrons, two or three atoms together would not have enough electrons to share to make all of the atoms stable. The best explanation for how metals form bonds is called the free electron theory. This theory says that metals share electrons on a grand scale. Thousands of atoms join together and electrons freely move from one atom to another to form stable atoms. This type of bonding is called metallic bonding and is shown in the picture above.

This free movement of electrons explains why most metals are good conductors of electricity. Compounds formed by metallic bonds also have

GOD'S DESIGN FOR CHEMISTRY
PROPERTIES OF ATOMS & MOLECULES

Atoms and Molecules

Elements

Bonding

Chemical Reactions

Acids and Bases

Biochemistry

Applications of Chemistry

Unit Activity & Conclusion

other similar characteristics. The free movement of electrons allows metals to conduct heat and gives metals their shiny appearance. They also have high melting points and are insoluble in water.

You can see that because elements can form ionic bonds, covalent bonds and metallic bonds, God has created elements that can produce a nearly endless variety of compounds. This is one reason why our world is so wonderful and so complex.

METAL MODELS:

Again, using marshmallows and toothpicks, make three or more beryllium models. Beryllium has 4 protons and 5 neutrons. It also has 4 electrons, two in its inner shell and two in its outer shell. After making the models, place the models near each other. Note that none of the atoms has enough electrons to be stable. Next, add some free electrons around the models. These represent the electrons that are shared freely among thousands of metal atoms in metallic bonds. Use the models made in the previous lessons as well as the ones made today to review the differences between ionic, covalent and metallic bonds.

WHAT DID WE LEARN?

What is the free electron theory? (It is the theory that metals form bonds by sharing electrons on a very large scale. Thousands of atoms allow their electrons to freely move about so that the atoms remain stable.)

How many valence electrons do metals usually have? (Usually 1, 2 or 3)

What are common characteristics of metallic compounds? (Free electrons, conduct electricity and heat, shiny luster, high melting point, insoluble in water)

TAKING IT FURTHER

Why don't metals form ionic or covalent bonds? (Because they have similar numbers of valence electrons, they do not pull electrons away from each other. Also, because they have a low number of valence electrons, they do not have enough to share among a small number of atoms. Therefore, they must share on a large scale—among thousands of atoms.)

Would you expect semiconductors to form metallic bonds? (No. Since they do not conduct electricity well, they would not have free electrons.)

Atoms and Molecules

Elements

Bonding

Chemical Reactions

Acids and Bases

Biochemistry

Applications of Chemistry

Unit Activity & Conclusion

LESSON 14

MINING AND METAL ALLOYS

MAKING IT STRONGER

SUPPLY LIST:

Tarnished silver object   Silver polish
Soft cloth

Most metals will form metallic bonds with other metal elements. However, most metal found in nature is not in a pure metal form. Most commonly, metal atoms combine with oxygen atoms to form metal oxides. To obtain pure metal from the metal ore, a chemical reaction must take place that will remove the oxygen from the metal ore. This type of reaction is called a reduction reaction. The process used to remove oxygen varies depending on the type of metal.

Many metals ores are purified through a process called smelting. For example, copper ore is smelted to reduce the amount of oxygen in it. The ore is crushed and heated. Then hydrogen is blown through the molten metal. The hydrogen combines with the oxygen in the liquid to form water; leaving nearly pure copper behind.

Further refining of copper is done by electrolysis. Carbon electrodes are used to pass an electrical current through the liquid copper. This allows any remaining oxygen atoms to combine with carbon atoms from the electrode to form carbon dioxide and allows the pure copper to collect on the other electrode. This results in nearly pure sheets of copper.

A similar process is used to produce pure aluminum. Bauxite is one ore that contains aluminum. It is dissolved in a cryolite solution, and then placed in an electrolysis set-up like the one shown here. The liquid aluminum collects on the bottom when electricity is passed through the solution.

Metals like copper and aluminum are very useful because they can then be molded into pipes or cans, or drawn into wires. However, pure metals are not always the best choice for a particular job. Scientists have found that by adding a small amount of another element to the molten ore, the resulting metal has superior qualities. For example, steel is iron with a small amount of carbon added. Steel is stronger and more flexible than iron.

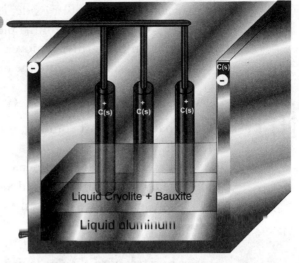

Liquid Cryolite + Bauxite

Liquid aluminum

To produce steel, iron ore is processed in a blast furnace. First, the ore is crushed. Then it is mixed with limestone and coke (a form of carbon—not the soft drink). This mixture is then heated to very high temperatures in a blast furnace. The resulting molten metal is called pig iron. This is iron with a significant amount of carbon in it. Pig iron can be cast into pots and other shapes, but it is brittle and is not useful for most other applications. To improve the quality of the iron, when the molten iron is removed from the furnace, oxygen is blown through the liquid where it combines with the carbon to form carbon dioxide, which bubbles out of the liquid. The remaining liquid is iron with just a small amount of carbon. This is called steel. Steel is pliable and strong and can be formed into rods, sheets and other shapes that are useful for many applications.

Other elements besides carbon are sometimes added to steel to further improve its performance. For example, chromium is added to produce stainless steel. This metal does not easily corrode so it is preferable for many applications, such as making forks and spoons to eat with. Another element that is sometimes added to steel is tungsten. Tungsten makes steel very tough. Tungsten steel is often used to make saw blades that last longer than regular steel blades. When a small amount of one metal is added to another metal the result is called an alloy. Alloys are often stronger, more resilient and easier to work with than the pure metal would be.

POLISHING SILVER:

When a metal combines with oxygen, an oxide is produced. Iron oxide is commonly called rust. Copper combines with oxygen to form a layer that is green instead of the shiny reddish-gold we commonly think of as copper. The Statue of Liberty is made of copper, but is green because the copper has oxidized. Silver also oxidizes. We usually say that silver has tarnished when the silver combines with oxygen. This oxidation leaves a streaky black surface on our silverware and other silver items. Because people prefer silver to be shiny and silvery, scientists have developed tarnish remover. Tarnish remover is usually a liquid or cream that combines

GOD'S DESIGN FOR CHEMISTRY
PROPERTIES OF ATOMS & MOLECULES

Atoms and Molecules

Elements

Bonding

Chemical Reactions

Acids and Bases

Biochemistry

Applications of Chemistry

Unit Activity & Conclusion

GOD'S DESIGN FOR CHEMISTRY
PROPERTIES OF ATOMS & MOLECULES

Atoms and
Molecules

Elements

Bonding

Chemical
Reactions

Acids and Bases

Biochemistry

Applications of
Chemistry

Unit Activity
& Conclusion

chemically with the silver oxide, leaving behind a shiny silvery surface.

Remove silver oxide from a piece of silver that is tarnished. Follow the directions on the tarnish remover. This will allow you to perform a chemical reaction and help restore the beauty of your silver at the same time.

WHAT DID WE LEARN?

What is the most common form of metal ore? (Most metals are in the form of metal oxides.)

What must be done to metal oxides to obtain pure metal? (The oxygen must be removed through a reduction reaction.)

What is an alloy? (A metal that has a small amount of another metal added to it)

Why are alloys produced? (Alloys are often stronger, more resilient and easier to work with than pure metals.)

TAKING IT FURTHER

Do you think chromium would be added to steel that is going to be used in saw blades? Why or why not? (Probably not. Chromium keeps steel from oxidizing; however, a little oxidation on a saw blade will not keep it from working. The saw blade needs to be strong, so tungsten may be added, but not chromium.)

Is oxidation of metal always a bad thing? (Not always. Sometimes a layer of oxidation prevents more oxygen from reaching the rest of the metal. So leaving a small amount of oxidation can actually reduce the overall amount of oxidation that occurs. This is not always the case, however; sometimes oxidation, such as rust, continues to occur until the sample is completely gone.)

CHARLES MARTIN HALL

(1863-1914)

Aluminum, believed to be the most common metal on earth, was discovered by Friedrich Wohler in 1827. This discovery, however, did not mean that aluminum was immediately available for use. In its natural state, aluminum is always tightly bonded with other compounds; most often it is in a compound called bauxite. Without an economical method for extracting the aluminum, pure aluminum was very expensive. During most of the mid 1800s, aluminum was so valuable that it was mostly used in jewelry and for special projects, like capping the Washington Monument. Because the unique properties of aluminum made it ideal for many applications, a race was on to find a less expensive way to extract it from the ore. Two men, working independently from each other, won this race. These two men, Charles Martin Hall of the U.S. and Paul Heroult of France, were born the same year (1863), made their discoveries the same year (1886) and died the same year (1914).

Charles Martin Hall was born in Thompson, Ohio, to Rev. Heman Hall and Sophronia Brooks Hall. When he was 10 years old, Charles and his family moved to Oberlin, Ohio. There he did his preparatory work in high school and, in 1880, began his studies at Oberlin College.

Charles did not take a formal chemistry class until his junior year in college; however, his interest in chemistry began much earlier. Hall met Dr. Frank Jewett, a well-educated chemist, while buying some equipment and chemicals during his first year of college. Hall and Jewett spent many hours discussing chemistry, and it is believed that Jewett was instrumental in encouraging and helping Hall in his discovery of aluminum extraction. In class, Jewett talked about the challenge of finding an economical method for extracting aluminum. Jewett said, "Any person who discovers a process by which aluminum can be made on a commercial scale will bless humanity and make a fortune for himself." Charles Hall took the challenge and told some of his fellow students, "I'm going for that metal."

Jewett, along with Charles' sister Julia, made many contributions to the discovery. Jewett let Hall use his laboratory in addition to the lab Hall had in the woodshed behind his own house. Jewett also supplied Hall with materials and up-to-date knowledge of chemistry. Jewett had gone to one of the best schools in Europe for his education, and before coming to Oberlin College, he taught at the Imperial University of Tokyo, so he was a valuable asset in Hall's quest for aluminum.

Charles' sister Julia had also gone to Oberlin College and had taken most of the same science courses he had taken. She was very involved in his research and probably helped him prepare many of the chemicals that he used. When he finally made his successful experiment on February 9, 1886, he repeated the experiment for Julia the next day, after she returned from a trip to Cleveland.

The famous experiment in 1886 used electrolysis to remove the aluminum from aluminum oxide. Hall accomplished this by dissolving aluminum oxide in a cryolite-aluminum fluoride mixture, then passing an electrical current through the liquid. The electricity caused aluminum to form and settle on the bottom of the vessel where it could not oxidize with the oxygen in the air.

Charles Hall applied for a patent for his aluminum reduction process in July, 1886, only to find that a Frenchman named Paul Heroult had already applied for a patent for the same process. How could two people in two different parts of the world come up with the same process at virtually the same time? These men were both very interested in solving this problem and had access to much of the same information and the same materials, so it is not surprising that they developed the same process. The patent dispute was resolved when it was confirmed that Hall had performed his successful experiment shortly before Heroult did.

Hall was very successful at overcoming obstacles and within a few years, he and his partners, with the possible help of his sister, were making commercial quality aluminum. In 1888, he and his partners started the Pittsburgh Reduction Company, and in 1907, the name of the company was changed to the Aluminum Company of America, which is today known as ALCOA.

By 1914, Hall's new process had caused the price of aluminum to drop from $12.00/lb. to $0.18/lb. As Jewett had predicted, Hall's discovery truly was a blessing to humanity and a fortune for him. Today, a host of items are made from aluminum. However, Hall did not keep all of his fortune for himself. He donated over $10 million dollars to Oberlin College. He also donated substantial amounts of money to Berea College, to the American Missionary Association and to educational programs in Asia and the Balkans.

Atoms and
Molecules

Elements

Bonding

Chemical
Reactions

Acids and Bases

Biochemistry

Applications of
Chemistry

Unit Activity
& Conclusion

CRYSTALS

SPARKLING LIKE DIAMONDS

LESSON 15

SUPPLY LIST:

Table salt
Epsom salt
Dark construction paper

2 plates
Scissors
Small pan

What do salt, sugar, sand, diamonds and snowflakes all have in common? They are all solids that have a crystalline structure. Certain materials form crystals when the liquid form freezes or becomes a solid. Crystals are solids whose atoms are in an orderly pattern. Crystals have flat surfaces called faces, and edges where their faces meet. There are seven major types or shapes of crystals. These are shown below:

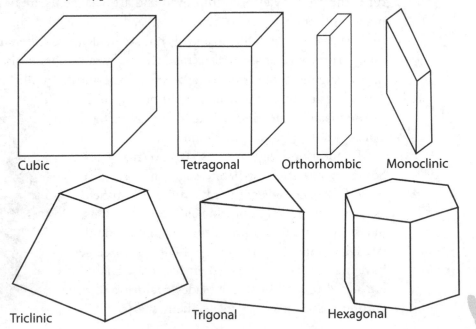

Cubic   Tetragonal   Orthorhombic   Monoclinic

Triclinic   Trigonal   Hexagonal

GOD'S DESIGN FOR CHEMISTRY
PROPERTIES OF ATOMS & MOLECULES

Atoms and Molecules

Elements

Bonding

Chemical Reactions

Acids and Bases

Biochemistry

Applications of Chemistry

Unit Activity & Conclusion

Large, perfectly formed crystals can only form when liquids are allowed to cool slowly and are not disturbed. This allows the atoms to line up in the crystal formation. If a liquid cools rapidly, crystals will not form at all, or only very small crystals will form.

The most common place to find crystals is among rocks and minerals. These compounds are the most likely to form crystalline bonds. One very common type of crystal is quartz. Quartz always forms 6-sided crystals. Another very interesting place to find crystals is in a geode. A geode is a rock in which crystals have formed in the center. A geode must be broken open to reveal the beauty of the crystals inside. Some crystals are made of only one kind of element. Diamonds, for example, are pure carbon. But most crystals are made from two or more kinds of atoms.

Other crystals form when minerals which have been dissolved in water crystallize as the water evaporates. Salt crystals often form this way. Crystals that form this way are also common in limestone caves. As water seeps through the limestone, it dissolves small amounts of calcite and gypsum. When the water drips from the ceiling of the cave, it slowly evaporates leaving behind the minerals as stalactites and stalagmites. These crystal formations can be very beautiful.

Not all crystals are formed naturally. The first artificial, or man-made, rubies were made in 1837, by a French scientist named Gaudin. Since that time, the process has been improved and artificial gems are now routinely made. Although some artificial gems, such as cubic zirconia, are crystals that are made to look like real gems but are made from different materials, many artificial gems are crystals made from the same chemicals as the naturally occurring gem. The elements are melted and then allowed to cool very slowly. Today over 44,000 pounds of artificial diamonds are manufactured each year, as well as artificial rubies, sapphires, spinets and emeralds.

In addition to gems, crystals have many uses. Some crystals, such as salt and sugar, are part of our food. Other crystals are used in the medical field as medications, and in hearing aids. Some crystals, like silicon, are used in the semi-conductor industry. Diamonds that are not good enough to be gems have many uses because of their hardness. Diamonds are added to drill bits, saw blades, scalpels and other cutting instruments to make them sharp and hard.

GOD'S DESIGN FOR CHEMISTRY
PROPERTIES OF ATOMS & MOLECULES

Atoms and Molecules

Elements

Bonding

Chemical Reactions

Acids and Bases

Biochemistry

Applications of Chemistry

Unit Activity & Conclusion

There are many other uses for crystals as well. God has blessed us with an abundance of crystals for a variety of purposes.

GROWING CRYSTALS:

You can make your own crystals by dissolving minerals in water and then allowing the water to evaporate slowly. This works best when you have a saturated solution. A saturated solution is one that cannot dissolve any more solute. The amount of solute that can be dissolved increases with temperature, so you will want to heat the water before dissolving the minerals.

You can grow two different shapes of crystals by doing the following:

1. Place a plate upside down on a piece of black or other dark construction paper. Trace around the edge of the plate. Remove the plate and cut out the circle. This will give you a circle of paper the same size as the plate. Place the paper on top of the plate.

2. Place ½ cup of water in a small pan and bring to a boil.

3. Dissolve as much table salt in the water as you can. Add the salt a teaspoon at a time until no more salt will dissolve.

4. Slowly pour the saltwater onto the paper on the plate until the paper is completely wet, but not soaked.

5. Place the plate in a place where it will not be disturbed.

6. Repeat steps 1-5 using Epsom salt instead of table salt

Allow the water to evaporate undisturbed for several days. After the water is gone, you should see crystals growing on the paper. The table salt crystals will be cube-shaped and the Epsom salt crystals will be long needles. When the paper is completely dry, look under the paper. There may be some crystals that formed under the paper as well.

WHAT DID WE LEARN?

What is a crystal? (A substance whose atoms are lined up in a regular lattice configuration. Crystals have smooth faces and defined edges.)

How do crystals form? (When a liquid cools slowly, the atoms line up in regular patterns to form crystal lattices based on their chemical characteristics.)

What is an artificial gem? (One that is formed by man and not formed naturally)

Where would you look to find crystals? (In rocks and minerals, in the kitchen—salt and sugar, in caves)

TAKING IT FURTHER

Why are naturally occurring gems more valuable than artificial gems when many are made from the same materials? (Even though they are made from the same materials, artificial gems do not have the same

53

GOD'S DESIGN FOR CHEMISTRY
PROPERTIES OF ATOMS & MOLECULES

Atoms and Molecules

Elements

Bonding

Chemical Reactions

Acids and Bases

Biochemistry

Applications of Chemistry

Unit Activity & Conclusion

strength and brilliance of naturally occurring crystals. God's crystals are still better than man's.)

Why is a saturated solution better for forming crystals? (The more atoms of the crystal forming material you have, such as salt, the more likely they are to line up in a lattice formation.)

What are some ways you use crystals in your home? (In food, in your computer, TV, phone, and other electronic devices, in your rock collection, gems in your mother's wedding ring, etc.)

FUN FACT

Salt has been a valuable crystal throughout history. Not only is salt used to season food, it has been used for centuries as a natural preservative. In ancient times, salt was so valuable that it was used as a form of currency. At times, people even preferred to be paid in salt rather than gold.

Atoms and Molecules

Elements

Bonding

Chemical Reactions

Acids and Bases

Biochemistry

Applications of Chemistry

Unit Activity & Conclusion

CERAMICS

MAKING IT WITH CLAY

SUPPLY LIST:

Polymer clay (Femo, Sculpey, etc.)

Crystals are an essential part of our lives. From computers to jewelry, we use crystals everyday. One very special type of crystal material is called ceramic. Ceramic comes from the Greek word for earthenware and describes where ceramics came from. Traditional ceramics include pottery, brick, porcelain and glass. And the common ingredient in each of these materials is clay, which comes from the earth—thus the name, ceramic.

The clay molecules in ceramic materials are fused with other chemicals by heat. The toughness, look and other characteristics of the ceramic material are determined by the crystal structures that are formed in the heating process. From the ancient Egyptians to the American Indians, people in many cultures have used the heating or firing process to strengthen their earthenware. People have been firing their pottery to make it stronger for thousands of years, long before anyone understood the chemistry behind it.

Today, with a better understanding of chemical bonding, scientists have developed advanced ceramics. These new ceramics are designed with specific, very pure substances that are fired in very specific ways to create very strong crystal structures. These new ceramics are replacing metal in many applications. The new ceramics are often stronger, harder and more heat resistant than the metals they replace. Also, ceramics are more chemically stable. They do not react with oxygen to form rust or other oxides like metals often do.

New ceramics are engineered for specific purposes. For example, special ceramic material is used to make artificial joints used in medical procedures. This new ceramic material contains calcium that will fuse with the surrounding bone; allowing the new joint to become part of the body.

GOD'S DESIGN FOR CHEMISTRY
PROPERTIES OF ATOMS & MOLECULES

Atoms and Molecules

Elements

Bonding

Chemical Reactions

Acids and Bases

Biochemistry

Applications of Chemistry

Unit Activity & Conclusion

Another special ceramic has been developed for use as heat absorbing tiles on the underside of the space shuttle. Ceramics are also being used as tools such as scissors, knives and blades for machines. As scientists learn more about chemistry, they will be able to continue developing more uses for special ceramics.

FUN WITH CLAY:

One of the most interesting new ceramics to be developed in recent years is polymer clay. Polymer clay is a special material that is soft and pliable. It can be molded into any shape and then remolded as often as desired. However, when the clay is baked at a low temperature, a chemical reaction occurs and the clay becomes hard. This clay is fun for children, but has recently become an art medium of its own.

Make a sculpture, beads, pots or other items using polymer clay such as Sculpey or Femo. Follow the manufacturer's directions for baking the finished masterpiece.

WHAT DID WE LEARN?

What is ceramic? (It is a material that is made using clay.)

What are some examples of traditional ceramics? (Pottery, brick, porcelain and glass)

What makes ceramics hard? (The material forms crystals when it is baked or fired.)

What are some advantages of modern ceramics? (They are hard, strong, heat resistant and don't rust.)

TAKING IT FURTHER

Why are the tiles on the space shuttle made of ceramic? (Because ceramic is very heat resistant, the tiles keep the heat generated by friction with the atmosphere away from the shuttle, allowing it to enter the atmosphere without burning up.)

Why are crystalline structures stronger than non-crystalline structures? (The lattice shape of the bonds allows atoms to be connected in more than one direction, so the compounds are stronger.)

BONDING QUIZ

LESSONS 11-16

For each characteristic below, write I if it describes an ionic bond, C for a covalent bond, and M for a metallic bond. Some characteristics have more than one answer.

1. _____ Formed by elements with very different levels of electronegativity

2. _____ High melting point

3. _____ Electrons are shared between two or three atoms

4. _____ Insoluble in water

5. _____ Forms ions

6. _____ Electrons are given up or pulled away

7. _____ Does not conduct electricity

8. _____ Sharing of electrons on a large scale

9. _____ Conducts electricity

10. _____ Flexible

Short answer:

11. How are crystals formed? _____

12. What is the smooth side of a crystal called? _____

13. What process is necessary for ceramics to become strong? _____

14. What is the common ingredient in all natural ceramics? _____

15. Name three traditional ceramics? _____

Atoms and Molecules

Elements

Bonding

Chemical Reactions

Acids and Bases

Biochemistry

Applications of Chemistry

Unit Activity & Conclusion

CHEMICAL REACTIONS

CHANGING FROM ONE THING TO ANOTHER

LESSON 17

SUPPLY LIST:

Birthday candle
Modeling clay
Jar

Vinegar
Baking soda
Matches

As you learned in the past several lessons, elements bond in many different ways depending on their electron structures. When two or more different elements bond together, a chemical reaction takes place and a new substance is formed. In a chemical reaction, the beginning materials are called the reactants and the ending materials are called the products. Some common chemical reactions you are probably familiar with include photosynthesis, bread dough rising, a flame burning or a firecracker exploding.

Chemical reactions often have a change of energy. If the reaction produces heat, the reaction is said to be exothermic. An exothermic reaction is one in which the products are warmer than the reactants. If the products are cooler than the reactants, the reaction is said to be endothermic; the reaction uses energy. Exothermic and endothermic reactions will be discussed more in a later lesson.

Sometimes chemical reactions are reversible. If water is broken apart into oxygen and hydrogen gas, the gases can later be recombined to form water again. Other chemical reactions cannot be reversed. For example, if you cook an egg, the egg cannot be "uncooked." Some chemical reactions happen very easily. You notice an immediate reaction when you combine baking soda and vinegar. Other reactions are slow or may even require heat, light or other stimuli to make them happen. For example, photosynthesis does not occur without sunlight and chlorophyll.

There are many different kinds of chemical reactions. If an element combines with oxygen, the reaction is called an oxidation reaction. If oxygen is removed from a substance, such as in the purification of metals, the reaction is called a reduction reaction. If elements other than oxygen combine to form a new substance, the reaction is a composition reaction, and if a substance is broken down into individual elements, the reaction is a decomposition reaction.

Some reactions happen very quickly. In fact, some are instantaneous, like the explosion of fireworks. Other reactions happen very slowly. A piece of iron, like this iron bucket, will eventually rust away, but depending on how much iron you start with, it may take years or even decades for the metal to all turn to rust. In order for a chemical reaction to take place, the reactants must be in contact with each other. So the speed of the reaction is not only affected by what kind of reaction is taking place, but also by the size and shape of the reactants. A cube of iron will rust much more slowly than a thin sheet of iron containing the same amount of material because the thin sheet has more surface area and the oxygen in the air can react with more of the iron molecules at one time.

Increasing the concentration of reactants will also speed up the reaction. The more molecules of each type of reactant there are, the more likely they are to come in contact with each other and react together. So adding more reactants or pushing them closer together will speed up the rate of the reaction.

In other reactions, heat can speed up the rate at which the reaction takes place. Heat causes the molecules to move more quickly so the reactants come in contact with each other more often and the reaction speeds up. Another way to increase the reaction rate of some chemical reactions is to add a catalyst. A catalyst is a substance that is added that encourages the reaction to occur, but is not used up in the reaction. We will explore catalysts more in a later lesson.

It is important to remember that chemical reactions are taking place all around us and even inside us all the time. These reactions are necessary for life and are designed by God to happen in a very predictable way. So enjoy learning about chemical reactions.

FIRE EXTINGUISHER IN A JAR:

A flame is a chemical reaction that requires oxygen. Therefore, it is an oxidation reaction. If you are trying to build a campfire, you need to make sure that air, which contains oxygen, can reach the wood, paper and other materials you may be using to build your fire. However, if a fire starts someplace you don't want a fire, one of the quickest ways to put out the fire is to deprive it of oxygen; the fire will then go out quickly. This is the way that many fire extinguishers work. The fire extinguisher sprays a chemical on the fire that keeps the oxygen away from the flames and allows the flames to go out.

GOD'S DESIGN FOR CHEMISTRY
PROPERTIES OF ATOMS & MOLECULES

Atoms and Molecules

Elements

Bonding

Chemical Reactions

Acids and Bases

Biochemistry

Applications of Chemistry

Unit Activity & Conclusion

You can build a fire extinguisher in a jar by doing the following:

1. Using a piece of modeling clay, attach a birthday candle to the inside bottom of a jar.

2. Pour ¼ cup of vinegar into the jar. Be sure not to get the wick of the candle wet.

3. Light the candle.

4. Sprinkle a teaspoon of baking soda into the jar. Be sure not to sprinkle it on the candle.

The candle will quickly go out, even though none of the ingredients you added touched it. The carbon dioxide produced by the reaction of vinegar and baking soda pushes the air out of the jar and deprives the flame of oxygen.

WHAT DID WE LEARN?

What is a chemical reaction? (When two or more elements combine together to form a new substance or when a substance is broken down into its separate elements)

What are the initial ingredients in a chemical reaction called? (Reactants)

What are the resulting substances of a chemical reaction called? (Products)

What is an endothermic reaction? (One that uses up energy—the products are cooler than the reactants.)

What is an exothermic reaction? (One that produces energy—the products are warmer than the reactants.)

TAKING IT FURTHER

How might you speed up a reaction? (Add heat, add surface area to the reactants by changing their shape—make them thinner or break or crush them, increase the concentration of the reactants, add a catalyst.)

A fire hose usually sprays water on a fire to put it out. Water does not deprive the fire of oxygen, so why does water put out a fire? (Water absorbs the heat from the fire, and heat is another necessary ingredient in producing and sustaining a fire.)

What is one chemical reaction taking place in the making of a loaf of bread? (The yeast reacts with the sugar in the bread dough to produce carbon dioxide.)

CHEMICAL FORMULAS

DESCRIBING HOW IT WORKS

Atoms and Molecules

Elements

Bonding

Chemical Reactions

Acids and Bases

Biochemistry

Applications of Chemistry

Unit Activity & Conclusion

LESSON 18

SUPPLY LIST:

1 copy of "Chemical Formulas Worksheet" per child (pg. 64)

Chemical reactions are taking place all around us, but it may be difficult to understand or visualize what is happening in a reaction. Therefore, scientists have developed a method for describing what is happening in a chemical reaction. This method is called a chemical formula.

Chemical formulas work just like mathematical formulas. When two quantities are added together in math, you can show that using an equation such as $4 + 3 = 7$. This equation tells you that if you add four apples to three apples you will end up with 7 apples. Similarly, a chemical formula tells you how different elements or compounds combine together to form new compounds. Chemical formulas use a + sign to indicate which compounds are combined or added together, but instead of an equals sign, chemical formulas use an arrow to show what the result is. The chemical symbol from the periodic table is used to represent each of the elements being combined. For example, below is the chemical formula for producing water:

$$H_2 + O \rightarrow H_2O$$

The small 2 next to the H means that 2 hydrogen atoms combine with 1 oxygen atom to make 1 water molecule that contains 2 hydrogen atoms and 1 oxygen atom.

The elements or compounds that are added together are called reactants, and the resulting compound is called the product of the reaction. In this case, the hydrogen and oxygen are the reactants and water is the product. This type of reaction, where two or more reactants are combined to form a single product is called a composition reaction. It has the general form of $A + B \rightarrow AB$.

GOD'S DESIGN FOR CHEMISTRY
PROPERTIES OF ATOMS & MOLECULES

Atoms and Molecules

Elements

Bonding

Chemical Reactions

Acids and Bases

Biochemistry

Applications of Chemistry

Unit Activity & Conclusion

Not all chemical reactions are composition reactions, however. Many reactions are just the opposite. If an electrical current is sent through a sample of water, some of the water molecules will break apart into separate hydrogen and oxygen gas molecules. This type of reaction is called a decomposition reaction. The general form for a decomposition formula is $AB \rightarrow A + B$. Notice that this format is the opposite of the composition reaction. The compound on the left is still called the reactant, but in this type of reaction there are two or more products. In the water example, water is the reactant and hydrogen and oxygen gas are the products. The formula for the decomposition of water is $H_2O \rightarrow H_2 + O$.

Chemical formulas can help us understand other types of chemical reactions as well. Sometimes a compound will combine with an element to form a new compound and a different element. This is shown by the chemical formula $AB + C \rightarrow AC + B$. In this reaction compound AB was broken apart. Then A combined with C leaving B by itself. This type of reaction is called a single displacement reaction. Element B was displaced by element C in the chemical bonding. The chemical formula helps us to visualize this reaction.

Another type of chemical reaction is called a double displacement reaction. This is demonstrated by the formula $AB + CD \rightarrow AC + BD$. In this type of reaction, elements B and C trade places, forming two new compounds.

It is important to note that whatever elements you start with must also end up on the other side of the formula. For a mathematical equation to be true, both sides must be the same. For example, if you place 4 apples in a bowl then add 3 more apples to the bowl, you will have the same number of apples as in a bowl with 7 apples; you will not have 6 or 8 apples. Similarly, for a chemical formula to be true, the number of atoms of each type of element must be the same on each side of the arrow. In the water formulas, there were two hydrogen atoms and one oxygen atom on each side of the equation. Below is the chemical formula for photosynthesis:

$$6\,CO_2 + 6\,H_2O \rightarrow C_6H_{12}O_6 + 6\,O_2$$

The 6 in front of the CO_2 indicates that 6 carbon dioxide molecules are needed for this reaction. Similarly, 6 water molecules are needed for this reaction. So, on the left side of the equation there are a total of 6 carbon atoms, 12 hydrogen atoms, and 18 (12 + 6) oxygen atoms. The carbon dioxide and water molecules are broken apart and the atoms combine to form one sugar molecule and 6 O_2 molecules. On the right side of the formula, there are 6 carbon atoms, 12 hydrogen atoms and a total of 18 oxygen atoms, just like there were to begin with. The First Law of Thermodynamics says that matter cannot be created or destroyed it can only change form. And chemical formulas help us to see that even though the product does not look at all like what you started with, the atoms, or matter, were not lost, their form was just changed.

Atoms and Molecules

Elements

Bonding

Chemical Reactions

Acids and Bases

Biochemistry

Applications of Chemistry

Unit Activity & Conclusion

CHEMICAL FORMULAS WORKSHEET:

Complete the "Chemical Formulas Worksheet."
Answers for the worksheet:
1. B 2. A 3. C 4. E 5. D 6. F 7. H 8. G
decomposition – 5, 7 composition – 1, 4, 6 single displacement – 3, 8 double displacement - 2

WHAT DID WE LEARN?

What is a chemical formula? (It is an equation that visually shows what happens to each element in a chemical reaction.)

What are the elements or compounds on the left side of a chemical formula called? (The reactants)

What are the elements or compounds on the right side of a chemical formula called? (The products)

TAKING IT FURTHER

What type of reaction is photosynthesis? (It is a single displacement reaction. The hydrogen atoms from the water molecules combine with the carbon dioxide in the formula.)

What is necessary for photosynthesis to occur that is not shown in the chemical formula? (Sunlight and chlorophyll are needed. Chlorophyll is not shown in the formula because it does not permanently combine with any of the reactants. It only speeds up the reaction. Chlorophyll is called a catalyst and you will learn more about catalysts in the next lesson.)

FUN FACT

When photosynthesis occurs, energy from the sunlight is stored in the sugar molecule. This is because photosynthesis is an endothermic reaction. When an animal eats the plant, the opposite reaction to photosynthesis takes place. The sugar in the plant combines with oxygen in the animal's body to produce carbon dioxide and water. The chemical formula looks like this: $C_6H_{12}O_6 + 6\ O_2 \rightarrow 6\ CO_2 + 6\ H_2O$. This is an exothermic reaction and releases the stored energy into the animal's body.

CHEMICAL FORMULAS WORKSHEET

A chemical formula is a way to describe what is happening in a chemical reaction. Remember that the elements on one side of the formula have to be the same as the elements on the other side of the formula.

Match the left side of the formula with the right side of the formula.

1. $4 Al + 3 O_2 \rightarrow$ A. $Li_2SO_4 + 2 H_2O$

2. $H_2SO_4 + 2 LiOH \rightarrow$ B. $2 Al_2O_3$

3. $4 NH_3 + 3 O_2 \rightarrow$ C. $2 N_2 + 6 H_2O$

4. $P_4 + 10 Cl_2 \rightarrow$ D. $C + O_2$

5. $CO_2 \rightarrow$ E. $4 PCl_5$

6. $H + OH \rightarrow$ F. H_2O

7. $2 KClO_3 \rightarrow$ G. $H_2 + 2 NaOH$

8. $2 Na + 2 H_2O \rightarrow$ H. $2 KCl + 3 O_2$

Extra Credit for older chemists:

Which of the above equations represent decomposition reactions? _____

Which of the above equations represent composition reactions? _____

Which of the above equations represent single displacement reactions? _____

Which of the above equations represent double displacement reactions? _____

Atoms and Molecules

Elements

Bonding

Chemical Reactions

Acids and Bases

Biochemistry

Applications of Chemistry

Unit Activity & Conclusion

CATALYSTS

SPEEDING THINGS UP.

LESSON 19

SUPPLY LIST:

Potato   Hydrogen peroxide
Apple   Lemon juice

As we have discussed in previous lessons, some chemical reactions are very quick and others are very slow. In order for many chemical reactions to take place, there must be a certain amount of energy available. You can think of it like climbing a mountain. The reactants have to reach a certain level of energy, or "height," before they can react with one another. However, adding another substance to the mix can sometimes speed up this process. This type of substance is called a catalyst. Adding a catalyst is like finding a pass or shortcut over the mountain. It reduces the amount of energy necessary for the reaction to take place.

We already discussed one very important catalyst—chlorophyll. Chlorophyll is a necessary ingredient in plant cells that helps speed up the reaction rate between carbon dioxide and water in the photosynthesis reaction. However, as we saw in the previous lesson, chlorophyll does not show up in the chemical formula because it is not used up in the reaction. A catalyst is something that alters the rate of the reaction without being consumed in the reaction. It is important to remember that a catalyst does not make an impossible reaction possible, it just makes the reaction easier. It can do this in a number of ways. Sometimes the catalyst bonds with one of the reactants to form an intermediate compound which then quickly reacts with the other reactant leaving the catalyst behind.

Some very important catalysts are called enzymes. Enzymes are found in living cells and are used in reactions involved in digestion, muscle contraction, cell construction and reproduction. Without the many enzymes in our bodies, the chemical reactions necessary for life would occur so

GOD'S DESIGN FOR CHEMISTRY
PROPERTIES OF ATOMS & MOLECULES

Atoms and Molecules

Elements

Bonding

Chemical Reactions

Acids and Bases

Biochemistry

Applications of Chemistry

Unit Activity & Conclusion

slowly that we would not be able to live. For example, in digestion starch is broken down into glucose. At normal body temperature, this reaction would take weeks to be completed. However, we cannot wait for weeks for our food to be digested. So God created the α-amylase enzyme to be part of our digestive systems. This enzyme makes it so the starch to glucose reaction takes only a few seconds.

Another common enzyme found in many living cells is catalase. Catalase allows the decomposition of hydrogen peroxide into water and oxygen ($2 H_2O_2 \rightarrow 2H_2O + O_2$) to occur nearly ten billion times faster than it normally would without it. This is very important because hydrogen peroxide, H_2O_2, is a byproduct of many cellular metabolic processes. This means that it is produced when your cells produce other needed chemicals. However, hydrogen peroxide is not a useful chemical in your body. So there needs to be a way to break it down into water and oxygen, two compounds that your body needs. Without catalase in your cells to break it down quickly, the levels of hydrogen peroxide would build up and poison your body. But God designed a way for the hydrogen peroxide to be quickly changed to useful compounds.

A catalyst can be very helpful if you wish to increase the rate of a reaction. But what if you want to slow down a reaction that is happening faster than you want it to? Food spoiling is a chemical reaction that we all want to slow down as much as possible. In this case you need a "negative catalyst." A "negative catalyst" is called an inhibitor. An inhibitor prevents a reaction from occurring by either keeping the reactants apart, or by bonding with one of the reactants so that the chemical reaction cannot take place.

OBSERVING CATALYSTS AND INHIBITORS:

Catalase is an enzyme that is present in many living cells. A simple way to observe the catalyst effect of catalase is to do the following:

1. Pour some hydrogen peroxide into a glass. Observe it for a few minutes. What do you observe happening? (Probably not much)

   A hypothesis is a good guess based on what you have learned. Make a hypothesis about what will happen if you place a slice of potato in the hydrogen peroxide.

2. Place a slice of potato in the peroxide and observe for a few minutes. What do you observe happening? (You should see little bubbles coming up off the potato. The potato contains catalase. The catalase is working as a catalyst to break the hydrogen peroxide into water and oxygen. The bubbles you see are the oxygen gas that is being produced.) Is this what you predicted would happen?

One common use of inhibitors, substances that prevent or slow down a reaction, is to prevent food spoilage. An easy way to observe the effects of inhibitors is to do the following:

GOD'S DESIGN FOR CHEMISTRY
PROPERTIES OF ATOMS & MOLECULES

Atoms and Molecules

Elements

Bonding

Chemical Reactions

Acids and Bases

Biochemistry

Applications of Chemistry

Unit Activity & Conclusion

1. Slice an apple into quarters.

2. Brush two slices of apple with lemon juice.

    What do you think will happen to the slices with the lemon juice? What do you think will happen to the slices without the lemon juice?

3. Wait 15 minutes. What differences do you see between the slices with the lemon juice and those without?

You should observe that the uncoated slices are turning brown and the coated slices are not. The acid in lemon juice acts as an inhibitor. It prevents the oxygen molecules from reacting with the apple molecules to produce the brown colored chemical. Other inhibitors are used in foods to prevent them from spoiling. They are often called preservatives on food labels.

WHAT DID WE LEARN?

What is a catalyst? (A substance added to speed up a chemical reaction?)

How does a catalyst work? (It reduces the amount of energy needed for the chemical reaction to take place.)

What is an inhibitor? (A substance that slows down or prevents a chemical reaction)

What is an enzyme? (A catalyst found in living cells)

TAKING IT FURTHER

Why is it important that living cells have enzymes? (If enzymes were not available, many chemical reactions such as digestion would take much too long to occur.)

Are catalysts always good? (Not necessarily. If a catalyst caused food to spoil very quickly that would be a bad use of a catalyst.)

FUN FACT

Nickel is a catalyst in the making of margarine. It is needed in the hydrogenation process that turns liquid vegetable oil into solid margarine.

Atoms and Molecules

Elements

Bonding

Chemical Reactions

Acids and Bases

Biochemistry

Applications of Chemistry

Unit Activity & Conclusion

LESSON 20

ENDOTHERMIC AND EXOTHERMIC REACTIONS

WHAT HAPPENS TO THE HEAT?

SUPPLY LIST:

5 eggs	Vinegar (room temperature)
Small pan	Thermometer
Timer	Jar with lid (Thermometer must
Steel wool (no soap)	fit inside the jar with the lid on)

Energy plays a very important role in chemical reactions. Without the energy from sunlight, photosynthesis cannot occur. The solar energy is stored in the sugar molecules and later released when an animal eats the plant. This storing and releasing of energy is a very important part of God's provision for life on earth.

A chemical reaction that stores energy is called an endothermic reaction. Another way to think of an endothermic reaction is to think of it as absorbing energy. The energy goes in and "in" sounds like "en", so endothermic has the energy going into the reaction. In photosynthesis, the energy that is absorbed is in the form of light. However, most endothermic reactions absorb energy in the form of heat. This energy must be added to the reactants in order for the reaction to occur.

One common endothermic reaction occurs when you are baking. Baking soda decomposes with the heat of the oven, releasing carbon dioxide gas. Similarly, yeast reacts much more quickly when heat is added. These are both endothermic reactions. One endothermic reaction you may not associate with heat is a chemical "ice pack." When an athlete is hurt, the doctor or trainer may use a special pack that contains two chemicals that are separated inside the pack. When these chemicals are combined, they absorb heat so the pack feels cool and helps reduce swelling around the injured area.

GOD'S DESIGN FOR CHEMISTRY
PROPERTIES OF ATOMS & MOLECULES

Atoms and Molecules

Elements

Bonding

Chemical Reactions

Acids and Bases

Biochemistry

Applications of Chemistry

Unit Activity & Conclusion

Not all chemical reactions absorb energy. Many chemical reactions release energy. These reactions are called exothermic reactions. You can remember this by thinking that "exo" sounds like "exit." The exit is how you leave a building, and energy is leaving an exothermic reaction. Energy can be released in the form of light or heat.

One of the most common examples of an exothermic reaction is combustion or burning. In one form of combustion, methane gas combines with oxygen to produce carbon dioxide, water, light and heat. The chemical formula for this reaction is $CH_4 + 2O_2 \rightarrow CO_2 + 2H_2O$. This is a similar reaction to the one between gasoline and oxygen in your car's engine.

The heat produced by combustion can be helpful if you are trying to heat your house, such as when you burn natural gas in your furnace. But in a car engine, too much heat can be harmful to the engine. Therefore, the engine must be cooled. This is most often done by running water from the radiator through the engine to absorb the heat.

Another very important exothermic reaction is the reaction that occurs as your food is digested. The energy released as food molecules are broken down is necessary for you to be able to function. The heat released helps your body regulate its temperature. Warm-blooded animals generally have to eat more food than cold-blooded animals in order to regulate their body temperatures.

OBSERVING ENDOTHERMIC AND EXOTHERMIC REACTIONS:

Endothermic Reaction:

An interesting endothermic reaction is one that occurs as an egg cooks. To observe the effect of heat on this reaction do the following. Label five pieces of paper with the numbers 1-5. Place 5 uncooked eggs in a small pan. Cover them with water and bring to a boil over medium heat. Begin timing as soon as the water begins to boil. After one minute remove one egg and place it on the paper marked with a 1. One minute later, after a total two minutes of boiling, remove a second egg and place it on the number 2. Continue removing an egg after each minute has passed, placing the egg on the paper showing its total cooking time.

After removing all of the eggs, remove the pan from the stove. Then break open each egg and you will be able to observe how the molecules in the egg have reacted as the heat was added to them.

Exothermic Reaction:

One reaction that produces or releases heat is the formation of rust. This occurs in small amounts and is not usually noticeable. However, you can measure the heat released in a sealed container. Place a piece of steel wool, the kind without soap in it, in a jar. Place a thermometer in the jar so that you can read the temperature in the jar. Seal the jar and wait 5 minutes. Read the temperature inside the jar.

GOD'S DESIGN FOR CHEMISTRY
PROPERTIES OF ATOMS & MOLECULES

Atoms and Molecules

Elements

Bonding

Chemical Reactions

Acids and Bases

Biochemistry

Applications of Chemistry

Unit Activity & Conclusion

Next, pour ¼ cup of vinegar over the steel. The vinegar must be at room temperature. The acid in the vinegar and the oxygen in the air will react with the steel to form rust. Reseal the jar and measure the temperature inside the jar every five minutes for twenty minutes. What did you observe? You should see the temperature in the jar rise as the chemical reaction releases heat.

WHAT DID WE LEARN?

What is an exothermic reaction? (A chemical reaction that releases energy)

What is an endothermic reaction? (A chemical reaction that absorbs energy)

TAKING IT FURTHER

If a chemical reaction produces a spark, is it likely to be an endothermic or exothermic reaction? (Light is a form of energy, so it would be an exothermic reaction.)

How does photosynthesis and digestion reveal God's plan for life? (Photosynthesis absorbs and stores energy from the sun in the sugar molecules in the plant. That energy is released during digestion after an animal eats the plant. This is God's plan for providing necessary food, and therefore energy, for all of the animals—and humans—on earth.)

If the temperature of the product is lower than the temperature of the reactants, was the reaction endothermic or exothermic? (If the result is cooler than the beginning reactants, then energy was absorbed, so the reaction was endothermic.)

CHEMICAL REACTIONS QUIZ

LESSONS 17-20

Mark each statement as True or False:

1. _____ All chemical reactions are fast.

2. _____ A catalyst speeds up a chemical reaction.

3. _____ Endothermic reactions use up heat.

4. _____ A fireworks explosion is an endothermic reaction.

5. _____ The same number of molecules must appear on both sides of a chemical formula.

6. _____ Chemical formulas demonstrate the 1st Law of Thermodynamics.

7. _____ Reactants are on the left side of a chemical formula.

8. _____ Catalysts are used up in a chemical reaction.

9. _____ Inhibitors speed up a chemical reaction.

10. _____ Sometimes inhibitors are helpful.

11. _____ Catalysts lower the energy required for a chemical reaction to occur.

12. _____ Exothermic reactions release energy.

13. _____ The product of an exothermic reaction is cooler than the reactants.

14. _____ Chemical reactions are rare.

15. _____ Heat can increase the reaction rate.

Atoms and Molecules

Elements

Bonding

Chemical Reactions

Acids and Bases

Biochemistry

Applications of Chemistry

Unit Activity & Conclusion

CHEMICAL ANALYSIS

WHAT IS IT MADE OF?

LESSON 21

SUPPLY LIST:

Red/Purple cabbage   Pan or microwavable bowl

How can you know what chemicals a substance contains? A good scientist always starts with observation. You can tell many things about a sample by observing its color, texture, state, mass, boiling and freezing points, and other physical characteristics. However, tasting and smelling chemicals can be very dangerous. Touching can also be dangerous as some chemicals are corrosive and can burn your skin. So direct observation of physical characteristics is limited. Therefore, often the most useful way to determine what kind of matter a sample is made of is to test it with chemical reactions. This type of testing is called chemical analysis.

Some chemical analysis techniques can be very involved and require a greater understanding of chemistry than we will cover in this book. Others are dangerous and should only be done in a laboratory. For example, one type of chemical analysis is called a flame test. A small sample of the substance is heated until it burns. The color of the flame can indicate what elements were in the sample. Other tests require expensive equipment. A spectroscope is a piece of equipment that passes a spectrum of light through a sample. The color of light that passes through indicates what the sample is made of. Although these tests are interesting, they are not easy to do at home. Fortunately, there are some chemical analysis tests that are fun and easy to do at home.

One common type of chemical test that is easy to do is to use indicators. An indicator is a chemical compound that changes color when it reacts with certain other chemicals. Iodine is a liquid that is normally red or orange-brown in color. But in the presence of starch, iodine reacts to form a liquid that is blue or green in color. This is a simple way to test if

GOD'S DESIGN FOR CHEMISTRY
PROPERTIES OF ATOMS & MOLECULES

Atoms and
Molecules

Elements

Bonding

Chemical
Reactions

Acids and Bases

Biochemistry

Applications of
Chemistry

Unit Activity
& Conclusion

your sample contains starch. Other chemicals change color when they are in the presence of protein or sugar. Indicators are an important part of chemical analysis.

One of the most common uses of indicators is to test for acids and bases. There are several chemicals that change color in the presence of an acid or a base. One of the most famous is litmus. Litmus is a chemical produced from lichen, a plant type of organism that is native to California. Litmus is naturally blue but it turns red in the presence of an acid. Blue litmus paper is thus used to test for acids in liquids. Once the paper turns red it stays red until it reacts with a base. Then it becomes blue again. So red litmus paper can be used to test for a base.

Other chemicals turn different colors depending on the strength or weakness of the acid or base. These chemicals can be dried together on one sheet of paper to form what is called a universal pH indicator. The pH scale, which stands for per hydronium, or power of hydrogen, indicates the strength of the acid or base. The pH scale goes from 0 to 14 with 0 being a very strong acid, 7 being neutral (neither acid nor base) and 14 being a very strong base. The universal indicator will change many different colors depending on the strength of the acid or base. A dark red reaction would indicate a pH of 1, orange would be a pH of 3, yellow would indicate a neutral solution, light green would be a pH of 10 and purple would indicate a strong base with a pH of 13 or 14.

If it is not critical to know the strength of an acid or base, other chemicals can be used just to indicate the presence of acids and bases. Bromothymol blue is a substance that is blue when acid is present, green when the sample is neutral and yellow in the presence of a base. Several plants can also be used to make acid/base indicators. One of the easiest to use is red cabbage. The liquid that is drained after boiling red or purple cabbage is purple. In the presence of an acid, it will turn pink and in the presence of a base it will turn blue.

Chemical analysis is very useful and can be fun. In the next few lessons, we will use an acid/base indicator to learn more about the chemicals around us.

MAKING AN ACID/BASE INDICATOR:

It is fun and easy to make your own acid/base indicator solution. Combine 1 cup of chopped purple cabbage with 1 cup of water. Heat in the microwave for 2-3 minutes or bring water to boil and boil for 5 minutes on the stove. Drain and save the water. The water should have a definite purple color. If the water is very light, add it back in with the cabbage and boil for a few more minutes.

The purple pigment from the cabbage chemically reacts with acids to form a pink liquid, and it chemically reacts with bases to form a blue liquid. If the substance is neutral, the indicator will remain purple. Use your new indicator to test several substances around the house to see if they are acids,

GOD'S DESIGN FOR CHEMISTRY
PROPERTIES OF ATOMS & MOLECULES

Atoms and Molecules

Elements

Bonding

Chemical Reactions

Acids and Bases

Biochemistry

Applications of Chemistry

Unit Activity & Conclusion

bases or neutral by combining a few drops of indicator with the substance to be tested. The substance to be tested must be a liquid or a solid that is dissolved in water.

Store your indicator in a sealed container and keep it in the refrigerator for future use.

WHAT DID WE LEARN?

What is chemical analysis? (Using chemical reactions to determine the composition of a substance)

List three different types of chemical analysis? (Flame test, spectrometer, indicators)

What is a chemical indicator? (A substance that changes color when is reacts with a specific chemical)

What is the pH scale? (The scale used to measure the strength of an acid or a base)

What does a pH of 7 tell you about the substance? (It is neutral. It is not an acid or a base.)

TAKING IT FURTHER

Why is it important to periodically test the pH of swimming pool water? (Water must be close to neutral to be safe to swim in. Also, water with a pH much greater than 6.8-7.0 can cause pipes to become clogged with minerals.)

Name at least one other use for testing pH of a liquid? (Hair treatments like permanents must be tested for pH so that hair curls and doesn't burn. Urine can be tested for pH to detect health problems. Beverages are tested for proper pH to ensure proper taste. Drinking water is tested for proper pH and wastewater is tested before releasing it back into the water system as well.)

FUN FACT

Hydrangeas are flowering plants. If the soil that the plant is growing in is acidic, the flowers will be blue. If the soil is basic, the flowers will be pink. Soil formed from chalk or limestone tends to be basic and soil formed from sandstone tends to be acidic.

FUN FACT

Stomach acid is hydrochloric acid and can be a 1 on the pH scale—a very strong acid. Lye, which is used in some cleaners and used to be used in soap, is a strong base and can be a 14 on the pH scale. Pure water, blood and eggs are a 7 on the pH scale. They are neutral.

Atoms and Molecules

Elements

Bonding

Chemical Reactions

Acids and Bases

Biochemistry

Applications of Chemistry

Unit Activity & Conclusion

ACIDS

LESSON 22

DOES IT BURN?

SUPPLY LIST

Lemon juice   Vinegar
Lemon lime soda pop   Milk
Cabbage indicator from lesson 21

What do you think of when you hear the word acid? Do you picture a liquid eating through metal and destroying everything in its path? Some acids are very caustic and can eat through metals; however, many acids are weak and are used every day. Let's take a look at what an acid actually is.

Acids and bases are substances that form ions when dissolved in water. Recall that ions are molecules or atoms that have either a positive or negative charge. When an acid is dissolved in water, one or more hydrogen atoms break off of the molecule. The original molecule holds tightly to the electrons so the hydrogen atom leaves behind its electron, causing the hydrogen to have a positive charge and the remaining molecule to have a negative charge.

The symbol for a positive hydrogen atom is H^+. The H^+ ion is really just a proton. It is very reactive and won't stay alone for very long. It quickly combines with a water molecule to form H_3O^+, which is called a hydronium ion. The formation of hydronium ions in water is what classifies a substance as an acid. Some acids are stronger than others. A strong acid easily gives up its hydrogen atoms to form hydronium ions and a weak acid holds onto its hydrogen atoms so it forms fewer hydronium ions.

Acids have specific characteristics. The word acid comes from the Latin word *acer* meaning sour, and foods that contain acids have a distinct sour taste. Citrus fruits have citric acid in them, which is why lemons and limes have such a sour flavor. Soft drinks containing carbon dioxide form car-

GOD'S DESIGN FOR CHEMISTRY
PROPERTIES OF ATOMS & MOLECULES

Atoms and Molecules

Elements

Bonding

Chemical Reactions

Acids and Bases

Biochemistry

Applications of Chemistry

Unit Activity & Conclusion

bonic acid, which gives the soda a sour/tangy flavor. Foods that contain vinegar, such as pickles, are sour because of the ascetic acid from the vinegar. And rhubarb contains oxalic acid, giving it a sour taste as well.

Acids also have other distinctive characteristics. Because acids easily form ions, they are good conductors of electricity. Most acids will react with metals and many are corrosive and can burn your skin. Acids neutralize bases. And finally, acids react with indicators. As discussed in the previous lesson, acids change the color of many different compounds when they are chemically combined.

Acids are found in many places other than food. Hydrochloric acid is found in your stomach and helps to digest your food. Sulfuric acid is used in car batteries. And decaying plants produce humic acid. So next time you hear the word acid, you don't have to fear a liquid that melts through everything it touches. Just think about your favorite soft drink.

TESTING FOR ACIDS:

In the previous lesson, you made some cabbage indicator that can be used to test for acids. Add a few drops of indicator to a sample of each of the following items to determine if they are acids.

1. Lemon juice

2. Vinegar

3. Clear soda pop—lemon lime works well

4. Milk

5. Saliva

What color did the indicator become when mixed with each of these items? Which items are acidic? (Should be lemon juice, vinegar, soda pop and saliva)

WHAT DID WE LEARN?

What defines a substance as an acid? (It produces hydronium ions when dissolved in water.)

What is a hydronium ion? (H_3O^+, formed by a water molecule and a hydrogen ion)

How is a weak acid different from a strong acid? (A weak acid holds onto it hydrogen atoms more strongly than a strong acid, so it forms fewer hydronium ions in water.)

What are some common characteristics of an acid? (Sour taste, conducts electricity in water, reacts with metals, many are corrosive, neutralizes bases, reacts with indicators)

How can you tell if a substance is an acid? (Dissolve it in water and use an indicator to test for acid.)

TAKING IT FURTHER

Why is saliva slightly acidic? (The acid in your saliva helps begin the digestion process by helping break down the food molecules.)

Would you expect water taken from a puddle on the forest floor to be acidic, neutral or basic? Why? (It would probably be acidic because the forest floor is covered with decaying plants and decaying plants produce humic acid.)

What would you expect to be a key ingredient in sour candy? (Some kind of acid. Sour spray and other sour candies often contain several types of acids.)

FUN FACT

Sulfuric acid is the most produced chemical in the United States. The biggest use of sulfuric acid is in the making of fertilizers. It is also used to make car batteries, paints, plastics and many other manufactured items. In fact, sulfuric acid is so important to manufacturing that some economists use a country's use of sulfuric acid as an indicator of how well that country's economy is doing.

FUN FACT

A bee sting contains formic acid. When the acid combines with the water in your skin cells it forms hydronium ions, which irritate or hurt your cells. You can help neutralize the acid from the bee sting by covering the area with a paste made from baking soda and water or with toothpaste.

Atoms and Molecules

Elements

Bonding

Chemical Reactions

Acids and Bases

Biochemistry

Applications of Chemistry

Unit Activity & Conclusion

Atoms and Molecules

Elements

Bonding

Chemical Reactions

Acids and Bases

Biochemistry

Applications of Chemistry

Unit Activity & Conclusion

LESSON 23

BASES

THE OPPOSITE OF ACIDS.

SUPPLY LIST:

Ammonia
Anti-acid tablets or liquid
Toothpaste

Soap
Baking soda
Cabbage indicator from lesson 21

A base is often described as the opposite of an acid, but what does that really mean? Just as an acid produces ions in a water solution, so also a base produces ions in a water solution. But an acid produces positive hydronium ions and a base produces negative hydroxide ions. When a substance that is a base is dissolved in water, it releases OH^- ions from its molecule, leaving the rest of the original molecule short one electron so it has a positive charge. The OH^- ion is called a hydroxide ion. The hydroxide ion is very reactive.

Just as the ability to produce hydronium ions determines the strength of an acid, so also the ability to produce hydroxide ions determines the strength of a base. The more hydroxide ions a base produces in water, the stronger the base. Weak bases hold onto their OH^- ions more tightly than strong bases do.

Another name for a base is an alkali. This is because some of the strongest bases are formed from the alkali and alkaline earth metal elements. These are the elements in columns IA and IIA on the periodic table. These elements include sodium, potassium and calcium.

Because of their common molecular structures, bases have common characteristics. One characteristic of a base is that bases have a bitter taste. Soap is a base and anyone who has ever gotten soap in his/her mouth can attest to its bitter aftertaste. Bases also have a slippery feeling. And because bases produce ions in water, they are good conductors of electricity. Many

GOD'S DESIGN FOR CHEMISTRY
PROPERTIES OF ATOMS & MOLECULES

Atoms and
Molecules

Elements

Bonding

Chemical
Reactions

Acids and Bases

Biochemistry

Applications of
Chemistry

Unit Activity
& Conclusion

bases are also caustic. A strong base can burn your skin as easily as a strong acid can.

Some common bases you may encounter include ammonium hydroxide which is found in many household cleaners, sodium hydroxide which is lye, and magnesium hydroxide which is found in anti-acid medications. The reason bases are used in anti-acid medications is that an acid and a base will neutralize each other. The H^+ from the acid will quickly combine with the OH^- from the base to form water. Another place you are likely to find a base is in your toothpaste. Your saliva naturally has acids in it that help digest your food, so toothpastes usually have a base in them to help neutralize the acid in your mouth to help prevent tooth decay.

TESTING FOR BASES:

You can use the cabbage indicator from the previous lessons to test for bases. Add a few drops of indicator to a sample of each of the following items to determine if they are bases.

1. Soap

2. Ammonia

3. Baking Soda

4. Anti-acid (liquid or tablets that are crushed and dissolved in water)

5. Toothpaste

What color did the indicator become when mixed with each of these items? Which items were bases? (They should all be bases. However, if you tested liquid soap and the indicator showed it to be an acid or to be neutral, check the bottle to see if it contains some kind of citric acid which is often added for scent.)

WHAT DID WE LEARN?

What defines a substance as a base? (It produces hydroxide ions when dissolved in water.)

What is a hydroxide ion? (OH^- ion)

How is a weak base different from a strong base? (A weak base holds onto its hydroxide ions more strongly than a strong base does.)

What are some common characteristics of a base? (Bitter taste, conducts electricity in water, feels slippery, many are corrosive, neutralizes acids, reacts with indicators)

How can you tell if a substance is a base? (Dissolve it in water and use an indicator to test for base.)

TAKING IT FURTHER

If you spill a base, what should you do before trying to clean it up? (Add an acid to neutralize it.)

Do you think that Strontium is likely to form a strong base? Why or why not? (Strontium is in the alkali metal family and alkali metals tend to form strong bases. Therefore, strontium is likely to form a strong base.)

FUN FACT

A wasp sting contains an alkali or base. When the hydroxide ions in the base irritate or hurt your cells, you can help neutralize the alkali from the wasp sting by covering the area with vinegar. But be sure that it is a wasp that has stung you and not a bee. Bee stings contain an acid and vinegar will only increase the problem, not neutralize it.

FUN FACT

Sodium hydroxide is a base that dissolves wood resin. It is added to wood pulp because it eliminates the resin, leaving the cellulose behind. The cellulose strands are then used to make paper.

Atoms and Molecules

Elements

Bonding

Chemical Reactions

Acids and Bases

Biochemistry

Applications of Chemistry

Unit Activity & Conclusion

SALTS

PASS THE SALT, PLEASE.

LESSON 24

SUPPLY LIST:

Lemon juice
Table salt

Anti-acid (tablet or liquid)
Swabs

What do you think of when someone says, "Pass the salt, please?" You would probably think of table salt. But sodium chloride, table salt, is not the only salt around. There are many other common salts. A few of these salts are used in cooking. For example MSG, monosodium glutamate, is a salt that is used in many oriental dishes. Other salts are used to make fertilizer, medical supplies and a number of other chemical products.

A salt is formed when an acid and a base mix. Recall that when an acidic material is dissolved in water the molecule breaks up into a positive hydrogen ion (H^+) and a negative acid ion. Similarly, when a base is dissolved the molecule breaks up into a negative hydroxide (OH^-) ion and a positive base ion. We already discussed how the hydrogen ion and the hydroxide ion combine to form water. But the positive base ion and the negative acid ion also combine to form a salt. For example, table salt is formed when a positive sodium ion, Na^+, combines with a negative chlorine ion, Cl^-, to form NaCl. Monosodium glutamate is formed when Na+ combines with the glutamate ion, $C_5H_8O_4^-$, to form $NaC_5H_8O_4$.

Not all acids and bases completely neutralize each other. When an acid and base do completely neutralize each other, the resulting salt is called a normal salt. But if some of the acid remains, the result is called an acid salt. If some of the base remains, the result is called a basic salt.

Because of their ionic structures, salts generally form crystals. If you examine table salt, you will see that it forms distinct crystal shapes. This is true of most salts. Another characteristic of most salts is the distinctive salty flavor.

GOD'S DESIGN FOR CHEMISTRY
PROPERTIES OF ATOMS & MOLECULES

Atoms and Molecules

Elements

Bonding

Chemical Reactions

Acids and Bases

Biochemistry

Applications of Chemistry

Unit Activity & Conclusion

Families of salts are named by the acid from which they originate. Sulfates are salts that are made from sulfuric acid. Chlorides come from hydrochloric acid. Nitrates are formed from nitric acid and carbonates come from carbonic acid. You may have heard of some of these salts and not realized what they were. Many fertilizers contain nitrates, phosphates and potash, which are all salts.

The next time you salt your corn on the cob, remember that there are many different kinds of salt.

WHAT IS THAT FLAVOR?

God designed different parts of the tongue to be able to taste different flavors. While the whole tongue can detect various flavors, some areas are more sensitive to certain ones than others The very tip of your tongue tastes sweet flavors best. To either side of the tip is the area that tastes salty flavors. On the sides of your tongue, you can taste sour flavors, and the back of your tongue is most sensitive to bitter flavors.

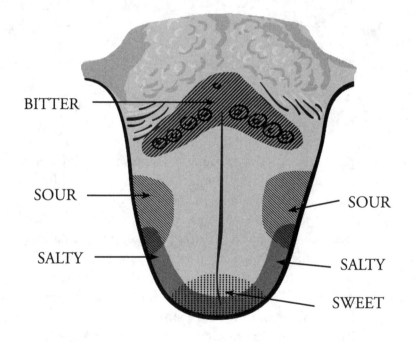

BITTER

SOUR

SALTY

SOUR

SALTY

SWEET

MAP OF THE TONGUE

Use a swab to apply a small amount of each of the following flavors to various areas of your tongue to test which parts of your tongue can detect each flavor.

1. An acid—use lemon juice
2. A base—use an anti-acid. If you have a tablet, crush it and dissolve it in a small amount of water.
3. A salt—dissolve table salt in a small amount of water.

GOD'S DESIGN FOR CHEMISTRY
PROPERTIES OF ATOMS & MOLECULES

Atoms and Molecules

Elements

Bonding

Chemical Reactions

Acids and Bases

Biochemistry

Applications of Chemistry

Unit Activity & Conclusion

WHAT DID WE LEARN?

Did you detect the various flavors in the areas indicated on the above tongue map?

How is a salt formed? (When a negative acid ion combines with a positive base ion, a salt is formed.)

What are two common characteristics of salts? (They have a salty flavor, and they form crystals.)

How are salt families named? (By the acid from which they are made)

Name three salt families. (Sulfates, chlorides, nitrates, and carbonates)

TAKING IT FURTHER

What do you expect to be the results of combining vinegar and lye? (You would get a salt and water.)

Why are some salts still acidic or basic? (The ions do not completely combine together, so some hydrogen or hydroxide ions are still present.)

If your tongue can only detect four different flavors, how can foods and drinks have so many different flavors? (There are many different combinations of acids, bases, salts and sugars in foods so there is a great variety. Also, flavor is not just what you taste on your tongue. It also includes the smell of the food as well.)

FUN FACT

Many paints receive their color from salts that are added. Vermilion is added to makes a red paint, cadmium sulfide makes a yellow paint and malachite is used in some green paints.

FUN FACT

Plaster of Paris, that white powder that is used for many art projects, is actually a salt—calcium sulfate.

BATTERIES

What do an eel, a ray, an African catfish and the Energizer Bunny's battery have in common? They all conduct electricity by chemical means. Chemicals have been used to generate electricity since Alessandro Volta produced the first battery in 1800. Volta discovered that stacks of copper and zinc that were separated by a salt-water solution would conduct electricity. This early battery was called a voltaic cell in honor of Volta and is the basis for all the batteries to follow.

At the heart of every battery is the electrolyte solution. An electrolyte is any solution that conducts electricity. Electricity is conducted by ions or charged particles, so solutions containing acids, bases or salts make good electrolytes.

In order to conduct electricity, a chemical reaction must take place inside the battery. A simple battery has a center core made out of graphite, which has a positive charge and is attached to the top of the battery. This core is surrounded by an electrolyte paste. The bottom of the battery is attached to a plate of zinc with a negative charge. When the positive and negative terminals are connected, electricity flows from the negative to the positive terminal through the electrolyte paste as a chemical reaction takes place.

Different types of batteries use different metals and different electrolytes, but the idea is the same. A very common example is the car battery, often called a lead acid battery. In a car battery, the negative plate, called the anode, is made of lead (Pb). The positive plate, called the cathode, is made of lead dioxide (PbO_2). These plates are submerged in a sulfuric acid solution (H_2SO_4). When the two plates are connected, the lead loses two electrons and becomes Pb^{2+}. This atom combines with an SO_4^{2-} ion in the solution to produce $PbSO_4$ (lead sulfate). At the cathode, PbO_2 atoms combine with the H_2 atoms in the electrolyte solution to form Pb (lead) and H_2O (water). This chemical reaction aids in the flow of electrons through the electrolyte solution which produces electricity that helps start your car.

In recent years, many new designs of rechargeable batteries have been developed. The batteries are recharged by applying a higher voltage in the opposite direction. This causes the chemical reaction to reverse and the battery can again produce electricity.

The next time you replace the batteries in your flashlight, remember that you are holding a chemical reaction in your hand.

ACIDS AND BASES QUIZ

LESSONS 21-24

Choose the best answer for each question.

1. _____ Which is not a type of chemical analysis?

    A. Flame test   B. Spectrometer   C. Indicator   D. Temperature

2. _____ pH indicators can tell the strength of which type of compound?

    A. Acid   B. Salt   C. Water   D. Tea

3. _____ What flower can indicate the pH of the soil by the color of its flowers?

    A. Rose   B. Hydrangea   C. Tulip   D. Daisy

4. _____ Which of the following is not an acid?

    A. Orange juice   B. Vinegar   C. Ammonia   D. Stomach fluid

5. _____ Which of the following is not a base?

    A. Saliva   B. Milk of magnesia   C. Soap   D. Lye

6. _____ What is formed when an acid combines with a base?

    A. Salt   B. Hydroxide   C. Hydronium   D. Balloons

7. _____ Which is not a characteristic of acids?

    A. Sour taste   B. Conducts electricity C. Corrosive   D. Slippery

8. _____ Which is not a characteristic of bases?

    A. Sour taste   B. Conducts electricity C. Corrosive   D. Slippery

9. _____ Which acid is the most produced chemical in the United States?

    A. Sulfuric   B. Hydrochloric   C. Formic   D. Ascetic

10. _____ What common product is made primarily from salts?

    A. Cake   B. Taffy   C. Fertilizer   D. Batteries

Atoms and Molecules

Elements

Bonding

Chemical Reactions

Acids and Bases

Biochemistry

Applications of Chemistry

Unit Activity & Conclusion

BIOCHEMISTRY

THE CHEMISTRY OF LIFE.

SUPPLY LIST:

Whatever food you have in your kitchen

Plants and animals depend on chemical reactions for nearly every function of life. As you have already learned, plants carry on the chemical reaction of photosynthesis, converting water and carbon dioxide into sugar and oxygen; thus providing food for nearly every food chain. Digestion is also a chemical reaction that breaks down the sugar into carbon dioxide, water and energy for the body. Another important chemical reaction that takes place in nearly every animal occurs during breathing. The hemoglobin in the red blood cells reacts with the oxygen in the lungs. This new compound is carried by the blood stream to all parts of the body where it reacts with the muscles to release the oxygen and make it available for other uses, such as digestion.

Chemical reactions are taking place in your body all the time. Most of these chemical reactions require water as a solvent. God designed the plasma in your blood to be mostly water, which is used to dissolve the many chemical compounds that your body needs so they can be easily transported throughout your body. About 2/3 of your body weight is water. This is about 70 pints of fluid in an average person.

Because water is so vital to most chemical functions in your body, it is necessary to make sure you drink enough water to replace the water used each day. Most people need about 4.4 pints of water each day. On average, 1.2 pints of water come from the food you eat, 2.6 pints come from the liquids you drink and the chemical processes that take place in your body produce about 0.5 pints of water. This should equal the amount of water you lose each day through urine, feces, sweat and breathing.

The major chemicals that are used by your body are proteins, fats and

GOD'S DESIGN FOR CHEMISTRY
PROPERTIES OF ATOMS & MOLECULES

Atoms and Molecules

Elements

Bonding

Chemical Reactions

Acids and Bases

Biochemistry

Applications of Chemistry

Unit Activity & Conclusion

carbohydrates. In order to be able to use these chemicals, your body produces over 50 different chemicals that are used in digestion. Most of these chemicals are enzymes, which are catalysts that are used to speed up the digestion process. The majority of these chemicals are supplied by the gall bladder, liver and pancreas. The chemical processes of digestion start in the mouth where the enzyme salivary amylase reacts with starch to break the starch molecules into sugar molecules. Once the food reaches the stomach, chemicals are added that break down proteins and fats. In the small intestine, more chemicals are added which break polypeptides, which come from proteins, into amino acids, and also break complex sugars into simple sugars. A multitude of chemical reactions are necessary for our bodies to function, and God designed each part of our bodies to perform the required chemical reactions in just the right way.

A BALANCED DIET:

Because your body needs particular chemicals to function, it is necessary that you eat a well balanced diet. You need to be sure to include carbohydrates, proteins and fats each day. To help you in deciding what to eat, food manufacturers include information on food labels that tell you how much of each of these chemicals you will get in a serving. The labels also tell how many calories are in a serving so you know how much energy the food contains. And because some people must watch their sodium intake, most food labels include the amount of sodium as well. The label shown here shows the chemical content for strawberry preserves.

According to the USDA (United States Department of Agriculture), each day everyone should eat foods from each

Nutrition Facts		
Serving Size 8 crackers (30g/1.1oz.)		
Servings per container About 5		
Amount Per Serving		
Calories 110	Calories from Fat 10	
		% Daily Value*
Total Fat 1g		1%
Saturated Fat 0g		0%
Polyunsaturated Fat 0g		
Monounsaturated Fat 0.5g		
Cholesterol 0mg		0%
Sodium 170mg		7%
Total Carbohydrate 23g		8%
Dietary Fiber Less than 1g		3%
Sugars 2g		
Protein 4g		
Vitamin A	0%	Vitamin C	0%
Calcium	0%	Iron	8%
Thiamin	15%	Niacin	8%
Riboflavin	8%	Folate	10%

* Percent Daily Values are based on a 2,000 calorie diet. Your daily values may be higher on lower depending on your calorie needs:

		Calories	2,000	2,500
Total Fat	Less than		65g	80g
Sat Fat	Less than		20g	25g
Cholesterol	Less than		300mg	300mg
Sodium	Less than		2,400mg	2,400mg
Total Carbohydrate			300g	375g
Dietary Fiber			25g	30g

Calories per gram:
Fat 9   •   Carbohydrate 4   •   Protein 4

of the following food groups: grains, fruits, vegetables, dairy and meat. This is because the various food groups are composed of the different chemicals your body needs. Grains, fruits and vegetables have the different carbohydrates your body needs. Dairy products and meats have proteins and fats.

Design a well-balanced meal that includes all the necessary chemicals to help your body stay healthy. Americans often eat foods high in fat and don't eat enough fruits and vegetables. Note that many pre-packaged foods contain a large amount of fat and salt—often more than your body needs. Fresh foods that you prepare yourself are generally healthier for you.

GOD'S DESIGN FOR CHEMISTRY
PROPERTIES OF ATOMS & MOLECULES

Atoms and Molecules

Elements

Bonding

Chemical Reactions

Acids and Bases

Biochemistry

Applications of Chemistry

Unit Activity & Conclusion

WHAT DID WE LEARN?

List at least two chemical functions performed by living creatures? (Photosynthesis and digestion. In plants, the equivalent of digestion is called internal respiration.)

What is the chemical reaction that takes place during photosynthesis? (Water and carbon dioxide chemically combine to form sugar and oxygen.)

What is the main chemical reaction that takes place during digestion? (Sugar and oxygen chemically combine to form carbon dioxide and water.)

What substance is necessary for nearly every chemical reaction in living things? (Water)

What are the three major chemicals your body needs that are found in the foods we eat? (Proteins, fats and carbohydrates)

TAKING IT FURTHER

Why did God design your body to have enzymes? (Enzymes help digestion and other metabolic processes to occur at a much quicker rate than they otherwise would.)

With what you know about chemical processes, why do you think it is important to brush your teeth after you eat? (The chemicals in your mouth begin the digestion process. These chemicals can cause tooth decay if they stay in your mouth too long. So you need to brush away any food and acids so your teeth stay healthy.)

Can you think of other chemical processes in your body besides the ones mentioned in this lesson? (Chemicals called hormones control your growth, chemicals are released to make you feel sleepy at bedtime, and taste and smell are chemical reactions. These are just a few examples. The list of chemical reactions in your body is very long!)

FUN FACT

Each day your body produces about 12 pints of digestion fluids. This includes 2.6 pints of saliva, 1.7 pints of bile, 2.6 pints of pancreatic juice and 5.1 pints of intestinal juices. Most of the fluid in these liquids is recycled throughout your body.

DECOMPOSERS

ULTIMATE RECYCLING

SUPPLY LIST:

Paper

Colored pencils

Have you ever thought about what happens to a plant after it stops growing and dies? Have you ever seen a dead animal beside the road and wondered what would become of it? God has provided a way for the chemicals that are in that plant or animal to be recycled. This process of recycling is called decomposition.

One of the most important elements that is recycled is nitrogen. Nitrogen is necessary for plant growth and plants absorb nitrogen from the soil. Some of this nitrogen is then absorbed into an animal's body when the animal eats the plant. If another animal later eats that animal, the nitrogen passes on to the larger animal's body. Once the animal dies, it then decays and the nitrogen is returned to the soil.

Consider what would happen if the plants and animals did not decay. The nitrogen in their bodies would be "lost" because it could not be reused, and eventually the earth would run out of nitrogen and new plants could no longer grow. Instead, there are special organisms to help break down dead plants and animals so that the nitrogen and other chemicals can be reused.

Scavengers are the first animals that help in the decomposition process. Scavengers are animals that eat dead animals. The most common scavenger is a vulture. But lions, bears, jackals, hyenas and komodo dragons are also scavengers. Sea sponges and insects are scavengers as well. Once the scavenger has eaten the dead animal, some of the chemicals become part of its body, but many of the chemicals are eliminated through its dung.

Organisms called decomposers then break down the nitrogen

Atoms and Molecules

Elements

Bonding

Chemical Reactions

Acids and Bases

Biochemistry

Applications of Chemistry

Unit Activity & Conclusion

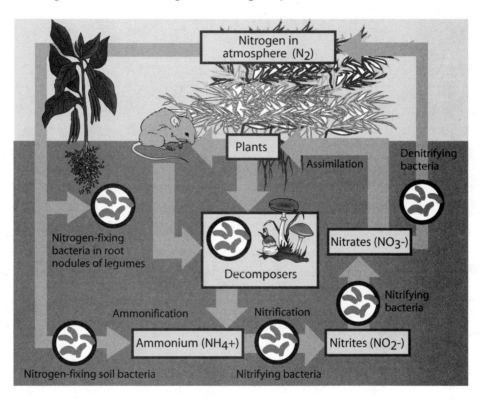

GOD'S DESIGN FOR CHEMISTRY
PROPERTIES OF ATOMS & MOLECULES

Atoms and Molecules

Elements

Bonding

Chemical Reactions

Acids and Bases

Biochemistry

Applications of Chemistry

Unit Activity & Conclusion

compounds and other complex chemicals in the animal waste into simple compounds. These decomposers are simple organisms like bacteria and fungi. Decomposers also work directly on dead animals and plants to break them down into elements that can be reused by plants growing nearby.

God created the first man, Adam, from the dust of the ground to live forever (Genesis 12:7). Adam's sin brought death into the world (Rom. 5:12) as part of God's curse on the world. Now when animals or people die, their bodies return to the dust of the ground (Gen. 3:19) and are recycled, like plants. God has even designed the affects of man's sin to be a blessing to the earth through the nitrogen cycle.

THE NITROGEN CYCLE:

Draw a picture of the nitrogen cycle. Begin with a picture of a plant in the center of the page, showing that nitrogen is being absorbed from the ground by the plant's roots. Then draw an arrow to a small animal, such as a mouse, that eats the plant. Next, draw an arrow to a larger animal, perhaps an eagle or an owl, that eats the smaller animal. The next arrow should point from the large animal to a scavenger, such as a vulture. From the vulture there should be an arrow to dung on the ground. This picture needs to be labeled as having bacteria. The final arrow should point to the plant, showing that the nitrogen has completed the cycle and is ready to be absorbed by a plant again.

Label the picture with the words "Nitrogen Cycle." This picture should demonstrate the path that nitrogen takes as it is used to support life on earth. Be sure to note that people absorb nitrogen when they eat plants as

GOD'S DESIGN FOR CHEMISTRY
PROPERTIES OF ATOMS & MOLECULES

Atoms and Molecules

Elements

Bonding

Chemical Reactions

Acids and Bases

Biochemistry

Applications of Chemistry

Unit Activity & Conclusion

well. The nitrogen cycle is God's plan for recycling nitrogen. In addition to nitrogen, other chemicals are recycled in a similar manner. Recall the carbon cycle you learned about in lesson 9.

WHAT DID WE LEARN?

What is a scavenger? (An animal that eats dead animals)

What is a decomposer? (An organism that breaks down dead plants, dead animals or dung into simple chemical compounds)

What is this way of recycling nitrogen called? (The nitrogen cycle.)

TAKING IT FURTHER

Why are decomposers necessary? (They are needed to break down complex compounds into simple compounds that can be used by plants. Without decomposers, the elements would be locked up and plants would not be able to grow.)

Were there scavengers in God's perfect creation, before the Fall? (No, there was no animal or human death before Adam sinned. Man and animals were all created to be vegetarians—see Genesis 1:27-31.)

Explain how a compost pile allows you to participate in the nitrogen cycle. (You can take food scraps, such as potato peels, and place them in a bin or pile outside. Bacteria, or other decomposers, eat these scraps, leaving behind compost, which is nutrient rich material that you can add to your garden. You have taken nitrogen from the food scraps and returned it to the soil to be used by the plants you grow in your garden.)

Atoms and Molecules

Elements

Bonding

Chemical Reactions

Acids and Bases

Biochemistry

Applications of Chemistry

Unit Activity & Conclusion

CHEMICALS IN FARMING

LESSON 27

HELPING PLANTS GROW

SUPPLY LIST:

2 identical plants – a fast growing plant like mint is a good choice
Plant food or fertilizer

As you learned in the last lesson, decomposers help nitrogen and other elements return to the soil to be reused by plants. This system works very well in natural areas. However, continuous farming of a piece of land uses up the nutrients, particularly nitrogen, faster than decomposers can replace them. In order to maintain healthy usable soil, the nutrients must be replaced.

There are several methods for replacing the nutrients in the soil. One of the oldest methods of keeping the soil viable is to use crop rotation. Different crops use nutrients in different amounts, and some crops, such as beans and alfalfa, actually return nitrogen to the soil, so planting different crops from year to year helps to keep the soil useful. Also, allowing a portion of the land to lie fallow, without crops, allows the bacteria in the soil to have enough time to return the needed nitrogen.

Crop rotation has been used for centuries. In the 19th century, parts of Europe, and England in particular, followed the Norfolk 4-course crop rotation plan. In the first year, the farmer would plant a root crop such as turnips. Year two, he would plant barley. Year three, he would plant grass or clover and allow animals to graze on it. Then, in the fourth year, he would plant wheat. Farmers repeated this cycle, and it helped to keep their land productive.

A second method for adding nutrients back to the soil is through fertilization. Nitrogen, phosphorous and other chemicals can be added to the soil in one of two ways. One way is through the application of animal dung. Much of the nitrogen that is in the plants that animals eat comes out

GOD'S DESIGN FOR CHEMISTRY
PROPERTIES OF ATOMS & MOLECULES

Atoms and
Molecules

Elements

Bonding

Chemical
Reactions

Acids and Bases

Biochemistry

Applications of
Chemistry

Unit Activity
& Conclusion

through the animal's waste. So, applying animal waste to the land is one way to improve the soil's productivity. A second way to add nutrients back to the soil is to add artificial or man-made fertilizers. These are chemicals that are prepared in a laboratory or factory and then applied to the soil.

The third method of improving the soil is through burning. This method is used primarily in tropical areas where the plant growth is rapid. Much of the nitrogen and other chemicals become tied up in unwanted plants that grow in the fields. Farmers burn these plants, and the ash returns the chemicals to the soil. Then the fields can be planted with desired crops.

Chemistry is important to farming in many ways other than just the nutrients in the soil. In fact, one type of farming does not use soil at all. Hydroponics is a type of farming in which plants are attached to some sort of supporting framework and the roots are bathed in a water solution containing boron, calcium, nitrogen, phosphorous, potassium and other chemicals. Hydroponics was first used on a large scale by US troops in the Pacific Islands during World War II. Canada began selling hydroponic tomatoes to the consumer in 1988. Today, it is often more economical to grow many flowers and vegetables using hydroponics than in the traditional manner. In this picture, strawberries are being grown hydroponically.

In addition to the chemicals needed by the plants, farmers also use chemicals as pesticides, fungicides and herbicides. Pesticides are chemicals that are used to control insects and other pests that might damage crops. Fungicides are chemicals that kill fungi and herbicides are chemicals that kill unwanted plants, like weeds, without damaging the desired crops. Researchers are always trying to find better chemicals to help crops grow without leaving behind chemicals that will hurt the consumer.

Because many people have concerns about eating crops that are treated with chemicals, some farmers have gone organic. This means that they grow their crops without the use of any artificial chemicals. These crops are often more expensive because the organic farmer has to deal with insects and weeds more than other farmers. But many people feel that organic produce is a healthier choice. You and your family will have to decide for yourselves.

Genetic engineering is another method that scientists are developing to help avoid the use of so many chemicals. Many crops have been modified with genes that make them resistant to certain diseases or undesirable to certain pests. Genetic modification can also make some crop plants more resistant to herbicides so only the weeds will be killed, but the plant will not be harmed,. A large percentage of produce in our supermarkets is genetically modified in some way.

THE EFFECTS OF FERTILIZER:

Obtain two identical plants. Prepare a solution of water and plant food according to the manufacturer's directions. Save this solution to use each day to water one of the plants. Label one plant as plant A and the other as

GOD'S DESIGN FOR CHEMISTRY
PROPERTIES OF ATOMS & MOLECULES

Atoms and Molecules

Elements

Bonding

Chemical Reactions

Acids and Bases

Biochemistry

Applications of Chemistry

Unit Activity & Conclusion

plant B. Pour ¼ cup of water on the soil of plant A each day. Pour ¼ cup of the water and plant food solution on the soil of plant B each day. If ¼ cup is too much or too little water to keep the soil moist but not soggy, adjust the amount as needed. However, be sure that both plants are receiving the same amount of liquid each time.

Based on what you have learned, which plant would you expect to grow faster? Why?

After a few days it should become obvious that the plant receiving the plant food is growing better than the plant without it. This is because the additional chemicals in the plant food provide the necessary nutrients for plant growth. If you did not see a significant difference, why do you think the plant growth was the same? (If the soil already had as much nutrients as the plants could use, adding more nutrients would not increase its growth. You can transplant both plants into less productive soil and try the experiment again.)

WHAT DID WE LEARN?

What are three ways that farmers ensure their soil will have enough nutrients for their crops? (Fertilizers, allowing the land to lie fallow, crop rotation, burning of unwanted plants)

What is hydroponics? (Growing without soil)

How are chemicals used in farming other than for nutrients for the plants? (Chemicals are used to kill pests, diseases and unwanted plants—pesticides, fungicides and herbicides.)

How is an organic farm different from other farms? (Organic farms do not use man-made chemicals)

TAKING IT FURTHER

Why did the farmers let cattle graze on their land once every fourth year in the Norfolk 4-course plant rotation method? (The animal waste added nutrients back into the soil.)

How does hydroponics replace the role of soil in plant growth? (A framework is provided to support the plants and nutrients are added to the water for absorption by the roots.)

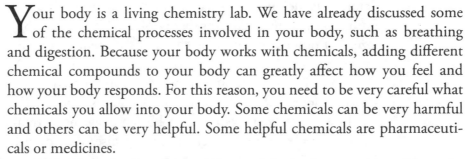

Atoms and Molecules

Elements

Bonding

Chemical Reactions

Acids and Bases

Biochemistry

Applications of Chemistry

Unit Activity & Conclusion

MEDICINES

HOW CHEMICAL COMPOUNDS AFFECT YOUR BODY

LESSON 28

SUPPLY LIST:

Bread

Garlic powder

Butter or margarine

Ginger ale

Your body is a living chemistry lab. We have already discussed some of the chemical processes involved in your body, such as breathing and digestion. Because your body works with chemicals, adding different chemical compounds to your body can greatly affect how you feel and how your body responds. For this reason, you need to be very careful what chemicals you allow into your body. Some chemicals can be very harmful and others can be very helpful. Some helpful chemicals are pharmaceuticals or medicines.

Herbs were the first plants to be used for healing purposes. Throughout history, people have used various plants as cures for different illnesses. Some have been more effective than others, but many have been very effective even if the user did not know why. Most herbal remedies were discovered by trial and error.

As far back as we have records, the bark of certain trees has been used to cure headaches. This remedy has been found in the records of the Egyptians, the Chinese and the Sumerians, as far back as 4,000 years ago. But it wasn't until the 19th century that scientists discovered that the tree bark contained salicylic acid, which today is the main ingredient in aspirin. The Bayer Company began selling aspirin as a medication in 1899.

The different effects of chemical compounds began to be studied in earnest in the 19th century, and since then many helpful discoveries have been made. In 1799, Sir Humphry Davy discovered that nitrous oxide could be used as an anesthetic to stop pain. Today we know this chemical as laughing gas, and it is frequently used in dental offices to eliminate the pain of

GOD'S DESIGN FOR CHEMISTRY
PROPERTIES OF ATOMS & MOLECULES

Atoms and Molecules

Elements

Bonding

Chemical Reactions

Acids and Bases

Biochemistry

Applications of Chemistry

Unit Activity & Conclusion

dental procedures. In 1831, chloroform was discovered and in 1842, ether was used during an operation for the first time. These and other anesthetic chemicals make it possible for doctors to perform operations without their patients feeling pain during the procedure.

When a patient takes a painkiller such as aspirin, or receives an anesthetic, the chemical in the medication locks onto the nerve cells in the brain. This prevents the pain signals from getting through, so the patient does not feel the pain. This process is like a chemical lock and key. The chemical is a key to locking up your pain receptors.

Shortly after these discoveries, many other drugs were discovered. The first synthetic, or man-made, drug was discovered in 1910. Then in 1930, a group of drugs called sulpha drugs was developed to kill some bacteria. But the really big break in medicine came in 1928, with the discovery of penicillin by Sir Alexander Fleming. Penicillin was the first antibiotic. An antibiotic is a substance produced by living organisms that is used to kill bacteria. Since the 1940's, dozens of other antibiotics have been discovered, such as amoxicillin and tetracycline.

In addition to antibiotics, another important medical use of chemicals is vaccinations. Vaccines are chemical solutions that have been developed to help stimulate your body's natural defenses against certain diseases. This helps to keep you from developing those diseases. Edward Jenner tested the first vaccine in 1796, when he gave an injection containing cowpox to people to help them develop immunity to smallpox.

The search for new medicines continues. A person who studies plants in order to develop new medicines is called an ethnobotanist. These scientists try to find plants with chemical compounds that are beneficial to the human body. Only about 0.5% of all plants in the world today have been tested for medical purposes. There may be many helpful substances that God has placed in the world just waiting to be discovered and used to benefit mankind.

Atoms and Molecules

Elements

Bonding

Chemical Reactions

Acids and Bases

Biochemistry

Applications of Chemistry

Unit Activity & Conclusion

COMMON HERBS:

Man has used herbal remedies for centuries. Ginger (shown at the right) is commonly used to settle an upset stomach. Certain oils have been used to improve digestion. Garlic (shown at the left) is a natural antibiotic and has been shown to help lower cholesterol. Ginseng is an herb that increases your energy level. The list goes on and on. You can enjoy the benefits of some of these natural herbal substances by making a fun snack of garlic bread and ginger ale.

Spread butter or margarine on a piece of bread. Sprinkle a small amount of garlic powder on the bread. Toast under the broiler of your oven until golden. Enjoy this natural antibiotic with a cool glass of ginger ale.

WHAT DID WE LEARN?

Why are chemicals used as medicines? (Your body is constantly performing chemical reactions, so adding chemicals to your body causes different reactions to occur.)

What were the earliest recorded medicines? (Herbs)

What was Sir Alexander Fleming's important discovery? (Penicillin—the first antibiotic)

TAKING IT FURTHER

If different plants have the potential of supplying new medicines, where might a person look to find different plants? (One of the likeliest sources of medicinal plants is believed to be the tropical rain forests where there are hundreds of unusual plants.)

What other sources might there be for discovering new medicines? (In addition to plants, animals in the rainforest and ocean are likely places to test for new medicines. Also, a better understanding of how the human body processes chemicals can lead to the development of new synthetic medicines.)

FUN FACT

Americans spend $5 billion each year on medicines that are derived from plants.

FUN FACT

Genetic engineers are working on developing new organisms that can quickly produce needed chemicals for medications.

ALEXANDER FLEMING

(1881-1955)

Alexander Fleming is a name you may not know, but you can be thankful for what he did. He discovered penicillin, a medicine made from a mold that kills harmful bacteria. Who was this man that would try such a thing? Alexander Fleming was born in Scotland in 1881, the seventh of eight children. The family worked an 800-acre farm where the children spent much of their time roaming the countryside. Later in life Alexander said, "We unconsciously learned a great deal from nature."

His father passed away when Alexander was 14. His oldest bother took over the farm, and Alec, as he was called, along with four of his siblings left Scotland and moved to London. After completing his schooling, Alec went to work for a shipping company, but he did not like it very much. So when the Boer War in South Africa broke out in 1900, Alexander and two of his brothers joined a Scottish regiment. This unit was never sent to war but spent most of its time playing different sports, such as shooting, swimming and water polo.

It was around this time that Alec's uncle died and left an inheritance of about 250 pounds to each of the Fleming children. Tom, Alec's brother, encouraged him to use his inheritance to study medicine. Alexander made top scores on the entrance exam and won a scholarship to St. Mary's, the school he preferred because he had played water polo against them. After completing his training, he could have left St. Mary's and taken a position as a surgeon. However, the captain of St. Mary's rifle club wanted Alec to stay and be part of his rifle team, so he encouraged Alec to switch from surgery to bacteriology, which he did.

In 1915, he married an Irish woman named Sarah Marion and they had a son who became a physician. When World War I started, Alec, and most of the people who worked in the lab he was in, went to France and set up a battlefield hospital lab. There on the battlefield he saw firsthand how small wounds could become infected and often lead to death. He felt that there must be some chemical solution that could help prevent this. He made many innovations in the treatment of the wounded during the war that helped improve the mortality rate, but he had yet to discover something that would prevent infection.

After the war, he spent most of his time researching different chemicals and made some important discoveries, but none as important as what he found in 1928. Fleming had been growing mold and bacteria in several different petri dishes. He had stacked several of them in the sink and did not get around to cleaning them up right away. When he finally did get around to cleaning up his experiments he looked at each one before putting it into the cleaning solution. One dish made him stop and say, "That's funny." In this dish, some mold had grown, and around the mold the staph bacteria had died. He sampled the mold and found it to belong to the penicillium family. He labeled his discovery penicillin.

He published his findings in 1929, but it raised little interest. Alec found it difficult to process the penicillin and a group of chemists took over the work for him. Eventually, even this work stopped when several of the chemists either died or moved away. Fleming's work on penicillin did not advance much more until Would War II started. At that time, Howard Florey and Ernst Chain started up the work again. They found a way to purify the mold and present it to the world.

In 1944, Fleming was knighted for his discovery, and in 1945, he shared the Nobel Prize for Chemistry with Howard Florey and Ernst Chain who finished the work that Alec had started. In 1947, Dr. Fleming became the director of the Wright-Fleming Institute of St. Mary's Hospital. He died at the age of 73 in 1955, and now rests in St. Paul's Cathedral in London.

Biochemistry Quiz

Lessons 25-28

Fill in the blank:

1. Identify two chemical reactions that sustain life. _____ _____

2. Name three main chemical compounds in food. _____

   _____ _____

3. What type of catalyst increases the rate of digestion processes? _____

4. What is an animal called that eats dead animals? _____

5. Name two types of decomposers. _____ _____

6. Name an element that is recycled by decomposers. _____

7. Name three ways to keep farmland productive. _____

   _____ _____

8. Who was the discoverer of penicillin? _____

Matching:

9. Kills unwanted insects   hydroponics

10. Kills unwanted plants   insecticide

11. Kills unwanted fungus   organic

12. Farming without man-made chemicals   herbicide

13. Growing plants without soil   antibiotics

14. Medicine to kill bacteria   vaccine

15. Medicine to encourage natural defenses   herbs

16. Some of these plants have natural medicinal value   fungicide

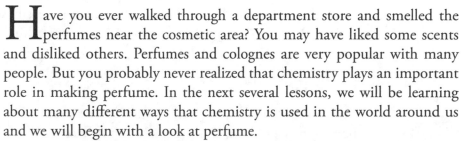

Atoms and Molecules

Elements

Bonding

Chemical Reactions

Acids and Bases

Biochemistry

Applications of Chemistry

Unit Activity & Conclusion

PERFUMES

WHAT'S THAT SMELL?

SUPPLY LIST:

Jar with a lid
15 whole cloves

Rubbing alcohol

LESSON 29

Have you ever walked through a department store and smelled the perfumes near the cosmetic area? You may have liked some scents and disliked others. Perfumes and colognes are very popular with many people. But you probably never realized that chemistry plays an important role in making perfume. In the next several lessons, we will be learning about many different ways that chemistry is used in the world around us and we will begin with a look at perfume.

A perfume is a liquid with a pleasant smell. It is aromatic; this means that its smell is easily detected by the human nose. In order for the liquid to be aromatic, it must contain scent molecules that are light enough to float in the air so they will reach the nose. These molecules must also be water soluble in order for the nerves in the nose to detect the scent.

Most perfumes are made by extracting scent molecules from plants that are considered to have a pleasant smell. Flowers are the most common source of scent molecules used in the making of perfumes. And this is where an understanding of chemistry becomes important.

The scent of a flower petal comes from the oil in the petals and this oil must be removed in order to make the perfume. There are two main methods for extracting these scent molecules from plants. The first is called solvent extraction. The flower petals are soaked in a solvent. The solvent is a chemical in which the oil containing the scent will dissolve. The flower parts are then removed. Next, the solvent is allowed to evaporate. This leaves the fragrant oil behind.

The second method of scent extraction is called steam distillation. In

GOD'S DESIGN FOR CHEMISTRY
PROPERTIES OF ATOMS & MOLECULES

Atoms and Molecules

Elements

Bonding

Chemical Reactions

Acids and Bases

Biochemistry

Applications of Chemistry

Unit Activity & Conclusion

this method, steam is passed through the petals causing the oil to vaporize. The oil moves with the steam through a tube to another container where both the oil and water condense and become liquids. The water sinks to the bottom of the container and the oil floats on the top of the water. The oil is then skimmed off of the water and removed.

Once the fragrant oil is obtained, the perfume is made by combining the oil with an alcohol. This is done so that the oil is easily sprayed onto your skin. The alcohol quickly evaporates, leaving behind the desired fragrance.

MAKING YOUR OWN PERFUME:

You can easily make your own perfume. Place about 15 whole cloves in the bottom of a jar. Next, add ¼ cup of rubbing alcohol to the jar and close the lid. Allow this solution to sit for 7 days. At the end of one week, remove the cloves from the alcohol and you have your own perfume. The perfume may not smell like cloves when you sniff the jar, but take a small amount of the liquid and place it on your skin. The alcohol quickly evaporates, leaving behind a pleasant clove scent.

WHAT DID WE LEARN?

What is a perfume? (A liquid with a pleasing smell)

What must be removed from flower petals to make perfume? (The fragrant oil)

Describe the two main methods for removing oil from flower petals. (With solvent extraction, a solvent is used to dissolve the oils, then the solvent is allowed to evaporate. With steam distillation, steam is used to vaporize the oil, then both the oil and water condense and the oil is skimmed off the top of the water.)

GOD'S DESIGN FOR CHEMISTRY
PROPERTIES OF ATOMS & MOLECULES

Atoms and Molecules

Elements

Bonding

Chemical Reactions

Acids and Bases

Biochemistry

Applications of Chemistry

Unit Activity & Conclusion

TAKING IT FURTHER

Why should you test a new perfume on your skin before you buy it? (The scent of the perfume in the bottle may not be the same as it is on your skin. The alcohol in the bottle may mask the true scent. So put some on your skin and see how it smells once the alcohol has evaporated.)

Why wasn't it necessary to use one of the methods described in the lesson to make your homemade perfume? (As the cloves soaked in the alcohol, the scent particles slowly moved into the alcohol from the cloves. This is a very slow process. The methods described in the lesson greatly speed up the process for commercial production of perfume.)

Atoms and Molecules

Elements

Bonding

Chemical Reactions

Acids and Bases

Biochemistry

Applications of Chemistry

Unit Activity & Conclusion

LESSON

30

RUBBER

DO YOU HAVE A RUBBER BAND?

SUPPLY LIST:

Balloon   Rubber band
Permanent marker

You place it on the end of your finger and slowly stretch it back; then suddenly you release it and it goes flying across the room! Who hasn't experienced the thrill of launching a rubber band? It's great fun to try to improve your aim and hit a target. (Just don't hit your brother or sister!) But did you know that there is a lot of chemistry involved in making a rubber band?

Rubber is made from a naturally occurring substance called latex. Latex is a sticky, milky colored material that is found in rubber trees. Rubber products became very popular in the early 1800s. However, two major problems occurred with the original rubber products. First, when the rubber got cold, like during a winter storm, it became brittle and cracked. Second, when the rubber got very warm, like in the middle of summer, it became sticky. Rubber products were not very useful if they could only be used in mild temperatures. A car with rubber tires wasn't' very useful if you could only drive it in the spring and the fall.

So scientists worked very hard to find a way to make rubber more useful. In 1839, a chemist named Charles Goodyear discovered how to improve rubber's performance. He found that adding sulfur to the latex caused it to become elastic and eliminated its bad reactions to extreme temperatures. This process was called vulcanization.

Rubber is a chemical that forms long chains of carbon and hydrogen molecules into what are called polymers. These linked molecules can pivot around the carbon atoms, allowing rubber to change it shape. Naturally, these long chains of molecules are a random mess. But when an outside

GOD'S DESIGN FOR CHEMISTRY
PROPERTIES OF ATOMS & MOLECULES

Atoms and
Molecules

Elements

Bonding

Chemical
Reactions

Acids and Bases

Biochemistry

Applications of
Chemistry

Unit Activity
& Conclusion

force is added, the chains can be stretched out and become parallel to each other. The chemical attraction of the covalent bonds pulls the molecules back into their original shape when the outside force is gone. Vulcanized rubber adds sulfur atoms to the polymer chains, connecting them together so that they act like one big molecule. This helps the rubber retain its elasticity, even at extreme temperatures.

Once vulcanization was discovered, rubber became very popular. People began trying to make nearly everything out of rubber. Of course, one of the most important uses for rubber was automobile tires. But clothing, shoes, balls, grommets, erasers and many other items were made of rubber as well.

This dependence on rubber became a real problem during World War II. After attacking Asia, Japan controlled most of the rubber tree plantations there, and the Axis powers together controlled nearly 95% of all natural rubber supplies. This created a crisis for America. To make a Sherman tank required ½ ton of rubber, not to mention all of the other rubber products required to keep an army functioning. So America did two things. First, the whole country did a major recycling campaign to provide enough rubber to keep the army going for at least a year or two. And second, the president asked scientists to develop an economical synthetic rubber.

Synthetic rubber had been discovered in 1875, but it was too expensive to make so it had not been developed. During World War II, it became crucial for the United States to find an inexpensive synthetic rubber. And that is exactly what the scientists did. And the process they discovered is still used today. First, scientists extract a chemical called naphtha from petroleum. Naphtha is then sent through a chemical process to change it into polymers that are very similar to natural rubber. This discovery helped America win the war and led to a boom in the number of uses for both natural and synthetic rubber.

Today, a large percentage of the rubber used around the world is produced from petroleum instead of latex from rubber trees. Synthetic and natural rubber are used in everything from automobiles to bikes, and from running shoes to clothing. Whether the rubber is natural or man-made, it is still fun to shoot a rubber band.

PLAYING WITH RUBBER:

Activity 1:

Most balloons are made from latex. This latex may be natural or synthetic, but it has the same effect. The polymer fibers of the balloon are all coiled up when it is deflated. As you inflate the balloon, the fibers are forced to stretch out and become straight. To see how this works, inflate a balloon, but do not tie it closed. Next, while you hold the balloon, draw a picture or write a message on the balloon (you may need someone to help with this step). Now, let the air out of the balloon and look at the picture. Has it changed? The stretched molecules have gone back to their original

GOD'S DESIGN FOR CHEMISTRY
PROPERTIES OF ATOMS & MOLECULES

Atoms and
Molecules

Elements

Bonding

Chemical
Reactions

Acids and Bases

Biochemistry

Applications of
Chemistry

Unit Activity
& Conclusion

shape and the picture has shrunk and changed shape along with it.

Activity 2:

Stretch a rubber band and quickly place it against your forehead. How does it feel? (It should feel warm.) Now remove the rubber band from your forehead and release the pressure on the rubber band, then quickly place it against your forehead again. How does it feel now? (It should feel cool.) The polymers release energy when they are stretched out so the rubber band feels hot for a few seconds after it is stretched out. The polymers gain energy when they recoil, so the rubber band feels cool for a few seconds after it returns to its normal shape.

WHAT DID WE LEARN?

What is natural rubber made from? (Latex from a rubber tree)

What is synthetic rubber made from? (Petroleum—oil)

What is vulcanization? (The process of adding sulfur to rubber to make it elastic in all types of weather)

What is a polymer? (A long chain of molecules connected together)

TAKING IT FURTHER

Why is it difficult to recycle automobile tires? (The vulcanization process makes the rubber very long lasting, but it also makes it hard to break down the molecules so recycling is difficult.)

What advantages and disadvantages are there to using synthetic rubber instead of natural rubber? (Synthetic rubber is cheaper than natural rubber; however, it requires petroleum, much of which America must import from other countries.)

FUN FACT

Synthetic rubber became widespread after World War II. In 1960, the use of synthetic rubber surpassed the use of natural rubber and this trend continues today.

FUN FACT

In 1943, James Wright was trying to produce a synthetic rubber, but only succeeded in producing a thick putty-like material. He put it on the shelf and forgot about it. A few years later a salesman picked it up and used it to entertain some customers. The value of the putty as a toy was soon recognized, and in 1957 it was introduced to the world as Silly Putty.

CHARLES GOODYEAR
(1800-1860)

The use of rubber is not new. The Indians of Central and South America were using it for centuries before Columbus found it and introduced it to western culture. The Indians called it "Caoutchouc" from the word "Cahuchu" which means "weeping tree." But the Europeans called it "rubber" because it could be used to rub out pencil marks, what today we would call an eraser. However, rubber did not have many uses until after 1839 because it had two main problems. In the heat of the summer it turned into a gluey mess and in the winter it became stiff and brittle. In 1839, this all changed, possibly by accident, but certainly through hard work.

Nine years earlier, Charles Goodyear, a bankrupt hardware merchant, walked into the Roxbury India Rubber Company in New York to sell them a new valve, but this company was also about to go bankrupt. The problem was that summer had come and all the products they had been selling were being returned because the rubber was melting. The directors, in an effort to keep things quiet, had even met in the middle of the night to bury $20,000 worth of the melting products in a pit. So Goodyear was unable to sell his valve. But after hearing this, Charles, at the age of 34, decided to take his first good look at rubber and to try to understand how it worked.

Since his trip was unsuccessful, he returned to Philadelphia and was put in jail for his debts. While in jail, he put his time to good use. He had his wife bring him some raw rubber and a rolling pin, and he did his first experiments with the gummy mess.

He tried adding drying powders like magnesia to the rubber with some promising results. And once out of jail, he, his wife, and their daughters made up hundreds of pairs of magnesia-dried rubber overshoes in their kitchen. Unfortunately, the heat of summer came before he could sell them and the overshoes turned into a shapeless paste. And the Goodyears were again penniless.

In addition, because his neighbors complained about Goodyear's smelly gum, he felt compelled to move. So he moved to New York. There, Goodyear tried adding two drying agents, magnesia and quicklime, to the rubber. After which he boiled the mixture. He was getting much better results, well enough that he received a medal at a New York trade show.

A further advancement came by accident. Charles put designs on the products he sold. And one time he used nitric acid to remove his design and found that it turned the rubber black. He threw this piece away only to retrieve it later because he remembered it also made the rubber smooth and dry. It was a better rubber than anyone had ever made. A business-man advanced him several thousand dollars to start producing this rubber. However, the 1837 financial panic wiped out the business and Charles and his family again lost everything. They ended up camping in an abandoned rubber factory on Staten Island and eating the fish they caught. But Goodyear did not give up.

Eventually, Goodyear moved to Boston and got backing to make mailbags for the government using his nitric acid rubber. He made 150 bags and left them in a warm storeroom while he took his family on a month long vacation. When he returned, he found a gummy mess on the floor of the storeroom. He still had not perfected the rubber process.

Goodyear again hit rock bottom and was dependent on the kindness of the farmers in Woburn, Massachusetts to give his children milk and half-grown potatoes to survive. Then he started using sulfur in his work with rubber. The details of how he made his famous discovery are not clear or consistent, but the most reliable story says that one cold day in February he went into the general store in Woburn to show off his latest gum-and-sulfur rubber when the customers sitting around the cracker-barrel started snickering at him. He must have been on very hard times because he was normally a mild-mannered man, but on this day he got excited and started waving a fistful of his gummy substance in the air. It flew out of his hand and landed on the hot potbellied stove and proceeded to cook. He went over to scrape it off the surface, thinking it would melt like molasses. Instead, what he found was a leathery rubber that had elasticity. This rubber was remarkably different from the other rubbers he had tried before; it was a weatherproof rubber. Goodyear denied this incident and said his discovery was not an accident.

That winter took its toll on Charles and his family. Due to failing health, he hobbled around doing his experiments on crutches. But he now knew that heat and sulfur held the answer he was looking for. The questions remained, how much sulfur, what temperature, and how long to heat it? After extensive experimentation, Goodyear at last found the right combi-nation of sulfur, heat and time. He found that pressurized steam at 270 °F for four to six hours gave the best results. This process is called vulcanization.

That spring, Goodyear went to Boston to find some old friends but found none. And he was jailed for non-payment of his hotel bill. Upon returning home, he found his infant son had died. In fact, only 6 out of his 12 children lived past infancy. Things looked very grim, but still Goodyear did not give up on his dream of producing a useful rubber.

He evidently wrote his wealthy brother-in-law about his discovery and his bother-in-law took an immediate interest in using the rubber as a textile. Two factories were put into produc-tion as the new form of rubber became a worldwide success. Unfortunately, Goodyear disposed of his manufacturing interest as soon as he could, and he never saw the millions he might have made.

Charles Goodyear was a good inventor, but not a good businessman. For instance, the people holding shirred-goods rights to his rubber made $3.00 a yard on the rubber they sold, while Mr. Goodyear made only 3 cents per yard. He was also in 32 different patent infringement cases. Some court cases went as high as the U.S. Supreme Court. In one of his cases, he hired Daniel Webster, at that time the Secretary of State, and paid him $15,000 to temporarily step down from office and work as his lawyer. This was the largest sum paid to a lawyer at that time. Mr. Webster's two-day speech won a permanent injunction against further patent infringements in the U.S. securing some rights for Goodyear. In spite of this victory however, Charles died in 1860, $200,000 in debt.

His family did eventually recover some of the royalties due them and eventually made a comfortable living. They finally reaped the reward for their father's undying commitment to the production of rubber. Today, we can't imagine life without rubber tiers, rubber boots and shoe soles, rubber seals, and a host of other rubber products; all because Charles Goodyear did not give up.

Incidentally, Charles Goodyear never had any connection with the Goodyear tire company that bears his name.

Atoms and Molecules

Elements

Bonding

Chemical Reactions

Acids and Bases

Biochemistry

Applications of Chemistry

Unit Activity & Conclusion

LESSON
31

PLASTICS

THE WONDER MATERIAL

SUPPLY LIST:

1 copy of "Chemical Word Search" for each child (page 113)

What would your life be like without plastic? Look around your home and notice how many items are made from plastic. Your mixer or blender, the handle on your refrigerator, buttons, light switch covers, even your clothes are probably made from some kind of plastic. Plastic is a modern wonder of chemistry. Since its discovery in the 1860s, plastic has revolutionized how many items are made.

Plastics are polymers. Polymer comes from the Greek words "poly" meaning many and "mer" meaning parts. A polymer is a giant molecule, which is really a long chain of molecules connected end to end. Many polymers occur naturally, including rubber, wool, silk and DNA. However plastic is a synthetic, or man-made, polymer.

The first artificial polymer was made in 1862. It was called celluloid because it was made from the cellulose found in cotton fibers. Later, polymers were made from coal tar. Today, plastic polymers are made from petroleum, or oil. The main ingredient is ethylene (a gas) which is combined with a catalyst that causes the molecules to form long chains. The first petroleum-based plastic was made in 1907. It was called Bakelite and was a dark brown moldable plastic that was mainly used for radio cabinets and later for TV cabinets or cases. Other famous plastics include nylon, which was invented by the DuPont Corporation in 1930, polyester, and acrylic.

One very interesting way that plastic is used is in the making of clothing. Polymer chips are melted. Then the liquid plastic is forced through very tiny holes and drawn into a thread. The thread is very thin and very flexible. This plastic thread is then woven into cloth to be used for clothing

GOD'S DESIGN FOR CHEMISTRY
PROPERTIES OF ATOMS & MOLECULES

Atoms and Molecules

Elements

Bonding

Chemical Reactions

Acids and Bases

Biochemistry

Applications of Chemistry

Unit Activity & Conclusion

and other products. Check the labels of your clothes and see how many of them contain polyester or nylon. Other man-made fibers include acetate and rayon, which are made from cellulose, not from petroleum.

Most plastics fall into two categories. One kind is thermoplastic. Thermoplastic is made by melting plastic chips, and then injecting the liquid into a mold. As the plastic cools it hardens and keeps its form. Thermoplastics will melt again if they are reheated. There are many uses for thermoplastics including trashcans and PVC pipe. However, it is very inconvenient in some uses for plastics to become soft or begin to melt when they become hot. Therefore, scientists have also developed thermosetting resin.

Thermosetting resin melts when it is heated initially. This liquid is placed in a mold under pressure in a process called compression molding. This kind of plastic hardens under pressure. Then once it cools, it will not melt again even if it becomes hot. This is much better for making items like coffee cups and baking dishes. Thermosetting resin is also used for car bodies and boat hulls, as well as a great number of other applications.

Today, millions of tons of plastic are produced each year. And the uses for plastic are innumerable. Plastics are used for counter tops, plastic bowls and cooking utensils. Plastics are also used in carpet and other floor coverings. Pens, paintbrush handles and many other art supplies are made from plastic. Plastics are used to make film. Plastics are used for fishing equipment and tricycles. And plastics are even used to make artificial joints for people. These are only a few of the many uses for plastics. If you look around you, you will find that plastics affect every area of your life.

CHEMICAL WORD SEARCH:

Using the "Chemical Word Search," review the meaning of each word then find the words in the puzzle.

WHAT DID WE LEARN?

What is plastic? (A substance made from polymers that are derived from petroleum.)

What is a polymer? (A long chain of molecules connected end to end)

What was celluloid, the first artificial polymer, made from? (From cellulose that comes from cotton plants)

What is the difference between thermoplastic and thermosetting resin? (Thermoplastics will become soft when reheated, thermosetting resin plastic will not.)

TAKING IT FURTHER

Name three ways that plastic is used in sports. (Plastic or vinyl balls, artificial rubber soles on running shoes, plastic hooks to hold soccer nets in place, polyester sports clothes and many other uses)

What advantages do plastic items have over natural materials? (Many

GOD'S DESIGN FOR CHEMISTRY
PROPERTIES OF ATOMS & MOLECULES

Atoms and Molecules

Elements

Bonding

Chemical Reactions

Acids and Bases

Biochemistry

Applications of Chemistry

Unit Activity & Conclusion

plastic items are stronger, more flexible and longer lasting than their natural counterparts.)

FUN FACT

Some plastics are ten times harder than steel.

FUN FACT

Petroleum is the main ingredient needed to make plastic. Petroleum is found in the ground under many parts of the world including parts of North and South America, Russia, Africa and the Middle East. But the largest deposits of oil are located under the ocean floor.

CHEMICAL WORD SEARCH

Find the following words in the puzzle below. Words may be horizontal, vertical or diagonal, including backward.

Polymer	Plastic	Rubber	Vulcanization
Perfume	Distillation	Synthetic	Alloy
Acid	Base	Salt	Indicator
Decomposer	Protein	Fat	Carbohydrate
Photosynthesis	Digestion	Atom	Bond

```
S  A  L  T  V  U  K  A  T  M  A  T  O  M  E
C  S  T  R  I  S  Y  N  T  H  E  T  I  C  I
C  P  E  R  F  U  M  E  O  R  E  A  D  F  U
A  E  S  S  A  K  T  V  I  X  Y  J  I  D  Y
R  P  H  O  T  O  S  Y  N  T  H  E  S  I  S
B  L  R  P  S  B  O  N  D  I  U  W  T  G  Z
O  A  G  O  W  T  H  E  I  S  C  N  I  E  M
H  S  U  L  T  B  N  M  C  D  F  H  L  S  I
Y  T  V  Y  N  E  W  B  A  S  E  B  L  T  Z
D  I  S  M  Q  U  I  I  T  A  T  T  A  I  S
R  C  R  E  J  E  P  N  O  B  L  I  T  O  M
A  R  K  R  E  B  B  U  R  C  A  L  I  N  Y
T  V  U  L  C  A  N  I  Z  A  T  I  O  N  S
E  A  A  C  I  D  D  H  G  Y  T  R  N  Y  O
W  P  R  U  F  R  E  S  O  P  M  O  C  E  D
```

Atoms and Molecules

Elements

Bonding

Chemical Reactions

Acids and Bases

Biochemistry

Applications of Chemistry

Unit Activity & Conclusion

FIREWORKS

Is it the Fourth of July?

LESSON 32

SUPPLY LIST:

Construction paper or tag board
Various colors of glitter
Glue

One of the most exciting parts of any Independence Day celebration is watching the fireworks display after the sun goes down. Fireworks have become an American Fourth of July tradition. But the earliest fireworks were the invention of the Chinese in the 10th century. These early fireworks were more like the later Roman Candles and were used in warfare rather than for entertainment. In 1242, an English monk named Roger Bacon wrote down the first European recipe for black powder, a key ingredient in fireworks. Then in 1353, the Arabs invented the first gun. But the first known use of fireworks for entertainment purposes was in France, when Louis XIV amazed his guests with fireworks sometime in the late 17th century. Later, the Italians added color to the fireworks and one of the most enjoyable forms of entertainment was born.

Making fireworks is a very specialized and somewhat dangerous use of chemical reactions. The recipe for each firework is unique. Most fireworks companies are family owned and the recipes for their fireworks are strictly guarded secrets, passed down from generation to generation. Still, there are some common steps in making and firing fireworks.

Each fireworks shell is packed with balls of chemicals. How the balls are packed determines how it will explode and what the explosion will look like. Different chemicals emit different colors when burned, so the type of chemical determines the color that will be given off. Sodium gives off a yellow light, copper salt produces blue, lithium and strontium salts

GOD'S DESIGN FOR CHEMISTRY
PROPERTIES OF ATOMS & MOLECULES

Atoms and Molecules

Elements

Bonding

Chemical Reactions

Acids and Bases

Biochemistry

Applications of Chemistry

Unit Activity & Conclusion

produce red and barium nitrate produces green.

The chemical balls are layered inside the shell and held in place by rice or corn. The shell is then wrapped in brown paper and paste and allowed to dry. Charges of black powder and fuses are then added to the shell. The charge on the bottom lifts the shell into the air. A bursting charge is added as well. Each charge has its own fuse, which determines when it will blow so that the shell does not burst before it reaches an appropriate altitude.

When the bursting charge explodes, the energy released excites the electrons in the outermost shell of the atoms, moving the electrons to a higher energy level than they would normally be in. This is an unstable situation so the electrons quickly go back to their original energy level. When the electrons return to their normal energy levels, they release energy in the form of light. Different chemical compounds release different wavelengths of light, thus we enjoy a wide variety of different colors of fireworks.

Nearly as much work goes into setting up a fireworks display as goes into making the shells. It can take up to two days to set up everything for a 30-60 minute fireworks show. First, copper pipes are used as mortars for firing the larger shells and PVC pipes are used to hold the smaller shells. One pipe is used for each shell to be fired. These mortars are set up and sand is packed around and in between each pipe to hold it in place. An appropriately sized mortar is set in each specific place according to the plan for when each shell is to be fired.

Next, a wire is run from a firing board to each mortar. The wire is then connected to the firing fuse of the shell. The firing board is then used to ignite each shell in the proper order. The size and order of each shell is determined ahead of time to guarantee a spectacular display.

Designing Your Own Fireworks Display:

Each firework has a special design to give just the desired effect. You can design your own fireworks display by making a fireworks picture. Decide the shapes and colors of the exploding fireworks and then draw the shapes on a piece of construction paper with glue. Next, sprinkle colored glitter on the glue and allow it to dry. Be creative and design fireworks that you would like to see.

What did we learn?

What are the key ingredients in a fireworks shell? (The chemical that releases the light, black powder for the explosion and fuses to light the powder)

Why does a fireworks shell have two different black powder charges? (One charge lifts the shell into the air and the other charge blasts the shell open.)

How do fireworks generate flashes of light? (When the blasting charge explodes, the energy released forces electrons in the chemicals into higher energy levels. When the electrons return to their normal energy levels, they release energy in the form of light.)

What determines the color of the firework? (The chemical compound that is packed inside.)

TAKING IT FURTHER

How can a firework explode and then change to a different color? (Two different chemicals are packed in the shell and ignited at different times.)

Why would employees at a fireworks plant have to wear only cotton clothing? (Nylon, polyester, silk and other fabrics can build up a static charge. This could be very dangerous when working around black powder because a static discharge could ignite the powder.)

FUN FACT

Fireworks are usually stored in bunkers that are separated by 20-foot mounds of sand. This way if one bunker somehow explodes, the others would still be safe.

Atoms and Molecules

Elements

Bonding

Chemical Reactions

Acids and Bases

Biochemistry

Applications of Chemistry

Unit Activity & Conclusion

Atoms and Molecules

Elements

Bonding

Chemical Reactions

Acids and Bases

Biochemistry

Applications of Chemistry

Unit Activity & Conclusion

ROCKET FUEL

DO YOU NEED A ROCKET SCIENTIST?

SUPPLY LIST:

- Balloon
- String
- Soda straw
- Tape

Have you ever watched the space shuttle lift off and fly into outer space? The engines ignite and steam and fire billow out the bottom as the shuttle lifts off the ground, picking up speed every second. This is an exciting thing to watch. And a lot of chemistry went into making the rocket fuel needed for that exciting lift-off.

Combustion is a chemical reaction that produces large amounts of heat. This reaction is what provides the thrust that pushes the rocket off the ground. In most modern rockets, the fuel of choice is the combination of liquid oxygen and liquid hydrogen. These two elements are kept under pressure and then combined in a combustion reaction inside the rocket engine. At very high temperatures the oxygen and hydrogen combust and turn into steam. The resulting gases are forced out the back of the rocket engine at very high speeds. The water molecules travel at about 560 meters/second. But not all of the hydrogen and oxygen atoms combine to form water; some atoms just evaporate and then leave the engine at high speeds, providing additional thrust. The O_2 molecules travel at up to 425 meters/second and the hydrogen atoms move at up to 1600 meters/second.

Newton's Third Law of Motion states that for every action there is an equal and opposite reaction. So, as the gases escape out the back of the rocket engine, they are pushing the rocket forward with the same amount of thrust. This is the basic physics behind a rocket.

Not all of the liquid hydrogen is used in the combustion reaction.

GOD'S DESIGN FOR CHEMISTRY
PROPERTIES OF ATOMS & MOLECULES

Atoms and Molecules

Elements

Bonding

Chemical Reactions

Acids and Bases

Biochemistry

Applications of Chemistry

Unit Activity & Conclusion

Because the reaction produces so much heat, some of the liquid hydrogen is piped around the inside of the engine where is absorbs heat to keep the parts from melting.

arlier rocket engines did not use liquid hydrogen and liquid oxygen as their propellants. Kerosene was one of the first rocket fuels. The gas produced in the combustion of kerosene is carbon dioxide. Carbon dioxide is heavier than steam so it does not move as quickly, thus it produces less thrust. Therefore, oxygen and hydrogen are more efficient rocket fuels.

The next time you see a video of the space shuttle taking off (or watch it in person), remember that the white clouds that are billowing around the shuttle are not smoke as you might think, but actually clouds of steam from the oxygen/hydrogen reaction.

BALLOON ROCKET:

You can't launch a rocket inside your house, but you can learn how rockets work by playing with a balloon. Blow up a balloon and then release it. What happens? The balloon goes flying around the room. This is because the air molecules inside the balloon are forced out the end. And as we already learned about motion, for every action there is an equal and opposite reaction. So, as the air molecules rush out the back of the balloon they are producing a force on the front of the balloon that makes it move.

To keep the balloon rocket from flying out of control, do the following:

1. Tape a straw to the balloon.

2. Thread a string through the straw.

3. Tape the ends of the string to opposite walls of a room or to two chairs that are several feet apart.

4. Blow up the balloon and pull it to one end of the string.

5. Release the balloon.

The balloon should fly forward along the string. You have now provided a guidance system for the rocket.

A real rocket has a very exact engine that carefully controls how the molecules exit the engine so that the rocket lifts off straight and does not fly all over the place like your balloon did.

WHAT DID WE LEARN?

What is combustion? (A chemical reaction that produces great amounts of heat)

What two elements are combined in modern rocket fuel? (Oxygen and hydrogen)

What compound is produced in this reaction? (Water/steam)

How does combining oxygen and hydrogen produce lift? (The reaction takes place at very high temperatures—heating the atoms to very high temperatures and thus very high speeds. These molecules exit the engine at great speeds, thus producing lift because of Newton's Third Law of Motion.)

What is Newton's Third Law of Motion? (For every action there is an equal and opposite reaction.)

TAKING IT FURTHER

Why can't we use oxygen and hydrogen to fuel our cars? (There are actually cars available that use hydrogen reactions to fuel the car, but a car does not need as much thrust or power as a rocket and rocket fuel is more dangerous than gasoline.)

Why is oxygen and hydrogen a better choice for rocket fuel than kerosene was? (The end product of the reaction of oxygen and hydrogen is steam and the end product of kerosene combustion is carbon dioxide. Water is lighter than carbon dioxide so it can move faster. The faster the molecules are moving when they leave the rocket engine, the more lift they produce.)

FUN FACT

The combustion reaction in the space shuttle's rocket engines lifts 4.4 million pounds (2 million kg) into orbit 290 miles (480 km) above the earth.

Atoms and Molecules

Elements

Bonding

Chemical Reactions

Acids and Bases

Biochemistry

Applications of Chemistry

Unit Activity & Conclusion

APPLICATIONS OF CHEMISTRY QUIZ

LESSONS 29-33

Briefly explain how chemistry is used in the making of each of the following items:

1. Perfume _____

2. Rubber _____

3. Plastic _____

4. Fireworks _____

5. Rocket fuel _____

Mark each statement as True or False:

6. _____ Vulcanization makes rubber useful in most temperatures.

7. _____ Rubber is made from cellulose.

8. _____ A polymer is a very short molecule.

9. _____ Today, synthetic rubber is more widely used than natural rubber.

10. _____ Perfume smells the same in the bottle as on your skin.

11. _____ Latex is a natural polymer.

12. _____ Bakelite was the first useful plastic.

13. _____ Plastic is an important product in American life.

14. _____ Fireworks are different colors because of different chemical compounds used.

15. _____ Recipes for fireworks are freely shared.

16. _____ Kerosene and carbon dioxide are common rocket fuels today.

17. _____ Newton's Third Law of Motion is important in rocket design.

18. _____ Combustion is a chemical reaction that produces large amounts of heat.

FUN WITH CHEMISTRY

UNDERSTANDING CHEMICAL REACTIONS.

Atoms and Molecules

Elements

Bonding

Chemical Reactions

Acids and Bases

Biochemistry

Applications of Chemistry

Unit Activity & Conclusion

LESSON 34

UNIT PROJECT SUPPLY LIST:

Milk (not skim)	Paper towels
Food coloring	Water soluble markers
Liquid dish soap	White glue
Disposable baby diaper	Liquid starch
Scissors	Plastic zipper bags
Eyedropper	

1 copy of "Fun With Chemistry Worksheet" for each child (pg. 124)

Now that you have learned about atoms and molecules, you should have a better understanding of what happens during chemical reactions. Take a few minutes to review what you have learned. Especially review lessons 17-20 on chemical reactions. Now, let's have some fun!

FUN CHEMICAL REACTIONS:

For each activity, complete the appropriate section of the "Fun With Chemistry Worksheet."

Activity 1: Moving Molecules

Pour one cup of milk into a dish. Place a drop of blue food coloring, red food coloring and green food coloring equally spaced around the edge of the dish. Observe the movement of the colors for several seconds. There should not be much movement. Now add a drop of liquid dish soap to the center of the milk and watch the movement of the colors. Write your observations and explanation on the worksheet.

Activity 2: More Moving Molecules

Fold a paper towel in half. Using a black water-soluble marker, draw a

GOD'S DESIGN FOR CHEMISTRY
PROPERTIES OF ATOMS & MOLECULES

Atoms and Molecules

Elements

Bonding

Chemical Reactions

Acids and Bases

Biochemistry

Applications of Chemistry

Unit Activity & Conclusion

one inch wide bar about one inch from the narrow edge of the paper. Draw a green bar and other colors of bars also one inch from the edge. Make sure none of your bars touch each other. Put about ½ inch of water in a sink. Carefully place the edge of the paper towel in the water so the bars are just above the water level. Set the paper towel against the edge of the sink and place a heavy object on the top edge to hold it in place. Allow the water to slowly wick up the paper towel for one hour. Observe the ink after one hour. Remove the paper from the water and allow it to dry. What did you observe about the ink? Write your observations on the worksheet.

Activity 3: Super Absorbent Molecules

You will be removing the powder that is found in an unused disposable baby diaper. During this activity be very careful not to inhale or swallow any of the powder and be careful not to get it in your eyes. Cut away the plastic outer covering of the diaper. Carefully place a large section of the inner padding in a plastic zipper bag. Wash your hands. Seal the bag and hold the padding toward the top of the bag and shake until you have about ½ - 1 teaspoon of powder in the bottom of the bag. Carefully remove the padding and discard it. Again, wash your hands.

Carefully pour the powder into in a large glass or mixing bowl. In a separate cup, combine one cup of water and a few drops of food coloring. Using an eyedropper, add the colored water one drop at a time to the powder. What do you see happening? After adding several droppers of water, begin adding water 1 teaspoon at a time. How much water do you predict the powder/gel will be able to absorb? See if you can add the whole cup of water to the gel. Write your observations on the worksheet.

Activity 4: Making Your Own Goop

Pour ½ cup of white glue into a mixing bowl. Add a few drops of food coloring if you desire. Stir in the food coloring until it is well mixed. Slowly add ¼ to ½ cup of liquid starch to the glue, mixing well until you have a gooey mixture that is easy to handle. What do you see happening? You can play with your goop. When you are done, place it in a plastic zipper bag for later playing. Wash your hands and record your observations on the worksheet.

EXPLANATION FOR EACH ACTIVITY:

Activity 1: Moving Molecules

Milk is a colloid; it is a liquid with solids suspended in it. Most of the solids in milk are fat molecules. These fat molecules keep the food coloring molecules separated from each other for the most part. When you add the soap, the soap molecules attract the fat molecules, allowing the food coloring to dissolve in the milk.

Activity 2: More Moving Molecules

This is an activity called chromatography. Black, green and many other

GOD'S DESIGN FOR CHEMISTRY
PROPERTIES OF ATOMS & MOLECULES

Atoms and
Molecules

Elements

Bonding

Chemical
Reactions

Acids and Bases

Biochemistry

Applications of
Chemistry

Unit Activity
& Conclusion

colors of ink are a combination of different colored ink molecules. These different molecules have different weights so they move up the paper towel at different rates. This allows you to see the different colors of molecules in the ink.

Activity 3: Super Absorbent Molecules

The powder in disposable diapers is a polymer called sodium polyacrylate. These molecules have the ability to absorb over 100 times its weight in water. This makes it very useful for diapers. This chemical is also used as a soil additive for some potted plants. These molecules absorb the water then slowly release it, allowing you to water your plants less often, and to use less water.

Activity 4: Making Your Own Goop

Starch and glue molecules combine to form a polymer. Recall that a polymer is a long flexible chain of molecules. This flexibility is what makes goop so much fun.

WHAT DID WE LEARN?

What was your favorite chemical reaction?
Why did you like that reaction?

TAKING IT FURTHER

What do you think will happen if you use skim milk in the first activity? (There are very few fat molecules in skim milk so adding the soap will make little difference. The colors will eventually mix, but at a much slower rate.)

What colors would you expect to see separate out of orange ink? Brown ink? (Orange is a combination of yellow and red. Brown is a combination of yellow, red and blue.)

Why is it important not to inhale the sodium polyacrylate from the diaper? (Evan a small amount of this chemical will absorb a lot of water, so it can irritate your lungs and your eyes by drying them out.)

Fun With Chemistry Worksheet

Activity 1: Moving Molecules

Beginning Ingredients	What I did	What I observed

This is why I think the colors swirled together after I added the soap: _____

_____

Activity 2: More Moving Molecules

Colors observed in the black ink	Colors observed in the green ink	Colors observed in the _____ ink

This is why I think the colors separated as they moved up the paper. _____

_____

Activity 3: Super Absorbent Molecules

Observations of powder before water	Observations of powder after adding water

This is why I think the powder changed its appearance. _____

_____

Activity 4: Making Your Own Goop

Observations of ingredients before mixing	Observations of ingredients after mixing

This is what I think happened in the chemical reaction. _____

_____

Atoms and Molecules Unit Test

Lessons 1-34

Use the Periodic Table of the Elements to complete the following chart:

Element	Symbol	Atomic #	Atomic Mass	# Electrons	# Protons	# Neutrons
	Fe					
Potassium						
		80				
					36	

For each pair of elements, write I if they are most likely to form an ionic bond, C for covalent bond, or M for metallic bond.

1. _____ Na + Cl

2. _____ H_2 + O

3. _____ O + O

4. _____ K + Br

5. _____ Al + Al

6. _____ Mg + O

7. _____ C + O_2

8. _____ Ag + Ag

9. _____ Cu + Cu

Use the words in the box below to fill in the blanks.

Catalyst	Enzyme	Base	Fat	Endothermic
Salt	Carbohydrate	Protein	Acid	Exothermic

10. A _____ can be used to speed up a chemical reaction.

11. The products of an _____ reaction have a higher temperature than the reactants.

12. The products of an _____ reaction have a lower temperature than the reactants.

13. An _____ is a catalyst that increases the rate of digestion.

14. An acid and a base combine to form a _____.

15. A substance is a/an _____ if it releases H^+ ions when dissolved in water.

16. A substance is a/an _____ if it releases OH^- ions when dissolved in water.

Draw a model of a helium atom, which has an atomic number of 2 and an atomic mass of 4.

Choose one of the following topics and briefly explain how chemistry plays a role in it:

Farming   Medicine   The Nitrogen Cycle

_____

_____

Matching:

17. Natural rubber is made from   Vulcanization

18. Synthetic rubber is made from   Latex

19. A long flexible chain of molecules   Combustion

20. Process that makes rubber strong and flexible   Petroleum

21. A natural polymer found in plants   Polymer

22. Process of burning that releases large amounts of heat   Cellulose

Explain the chemical reaction involved in your favorite experiment from this book.

_____

_____

_____

Atoms and
Molecules

Elements

Bonding

Chemical
Reactions

Acids and Bases

Biochemistry

Applications of
Chemistry

Unit Activity
& Conclusion

CONCLUSION

APPRECIATING OUR ORDERLY UNIVERSE

LESSON 35

SUPPLY LIST:

Bible

We live in a world that operates according to specific natural laws that were set in motion by God. We have learned how God designed our world to recycle all of the elements so that the matter in the universe is not used up. God designed our bodies to perform chemical reactions that are complementary to the reactions performed by plants; plants provide food and oxygen for us, and we provide carbon dioxide for photosynthesis.

All that you have learned about chemistry should point out that God is the master designer of our world. So take a few minutes to reflect on God's design of our world.

REFLECTING ON GOD'S WONDERFUL CREATION:

Take a few minutes to read some scripture verses that describe God's work in our world. Read Psalm 148, Isaiah 42:5-7, Colossians1:16-17 and Job 42:1-2

Now take a few moments and thank God for creating a world that obeys his rules, even at the molecular and atomic levels.

APPENDIX A
ANSWERS TO QUIZZES AND TEST

ATOMS AND MOLECULES QUIZ ANSWERS:

A. Electron B. Proton or neutron C. Neutron or proton B and C together – Nucleus
1. matter 2. proton 3. electron 4. neutron 5. valence electrons 6. nucleus 7. diatomic molecule
8. atom 9. atomic number 10. molecule

Element	Atomic #	Atomic Mass	# of protons	# electrons	# neutrons
Carbon	6	12.01	6	6	6
Aluminum	13	26.98	13	13	14
Tungsten	74	183.9	74	74	110

ELEMENTS QUIZ ANSWERS:

1. The same number of valence electrons. 2. Electrons filling the same energy levels 3. VIIIA 4.
IIA 5. IA 6. Metal 7. Metal 8. Metal 9. Non-metal 10. Metal 11. Non-metal
12. Metalloid 13. Non-metal 14. Metalloid 15. Metal 16. T 17. F 18. T 19. T 20. F 21. T 22. T

BONDING QUIZ ANSWERS:

1. I 2. I, M 3. C 4. C, M 5. I 6. I 7. C 8. M 9. I, M 10. C 11. When a liquid slowly cools the
atoms may line up in specific patterns to form crystals. 12. A face 13. Heating or firing 14.
Clay 15. Pottery, brick, porcelain, glass

CHEMICAL REACTIONS QUIZ ANSWERS:

1. F 2. T 3. T 4. F 5. T 6. T 7. T 8. F 9. F 10. T 11. T 12. T 13. F 14. F 15. T

ACIDS AND BASES QUIZ ANSWERS:

1. D 2. A 3. B 4. C 5. A 6. A 7. D 8. A 9. A 10. C

BIOCHEMISTRY QUIZ ANSWERS:

1. photosynthesis, digestion 2. carbohydrates, proteins, fat 3. enzymes 4. decomposer
5. bacteria, fungi 6. nitrogen 7. crop rotation, lying fallow, fertilizers 8. Alexander Fleming 9.
insecticide 10. herbicide 11. fungicide 12. organic 13. hydroponics
14. antibiotics 15. vaccine 16. herbs

APPLICATIONS OF CHEMISTRY QUIZ ANSWERS:

1. Solvent extraction or steam distillation is used to extract the scent molecules from flowers. These are then combined with alcohol to form perfume. 2. Sulfur is added to rubber and then the mixture is heated to form molecules that are strong and flexible. 3. Long flexible polymers are formed from petroleum, and then heated and molded into plastic. 4. Energy is added to chemical compounds to excite the electrons. When electrons return to their normal levels, they release light. Chemistry is also used in the combustion reaction of the black powder. 5. Liquid hydrogen and oxygen are combined at high temperature to produce the combustion reaction that provides the needed thrust for lifting a rocket.

6. T 7. F 8. F 9. T 10. F 11. T 12. T 13. T 14. T 15. F 16. F 17. T 18. T

ATOMS AND MOLECULES UNIT TEST ANSWERS:

Element	Symbol	Atomic #	Atomic Mass	# Electrons	# Protons	# Neutrons
Iron	Fe	26	55.85	26	26	30
Potassium	K	19	39.1	19	19	20
Mercury	Hg	80	200.5	80	80	120 or 121
Krypton	Kr	36	83.8	36	36	48

1. I 2. C 3. C 4. I 5. M 6. I 7. C 8. M 9. M Note: elements on opposite sides of the periodic table are likely to form ionic bonds, elements that are both metals (from the left side) will form metallic bonds, elements from the right side (non-metals) usually form covalent bonds. 10. catalyst 11. exothermic 12. endothermic 13. enzyme 14. salt

15. acid 16. base

Helium

Farming: Nitrogen and other chemicals are used up in the growing of crops so chemical fertilizers or other methods must be used to replace them. Also, insecticides, herbicides and fungicides are all chemicals used to improve crop yield. Medicine: Chemicals are used to change the chemical reactions in the body to improve health. Nitrogen Cycle: Nitrogen is used by plants, passed on to animals for their use, and then returned to the soil by decomposers.

17. Latex 18. Petroleum 19. Polymer 20. Vulcanization 21. Cellulose 22. Combustion

APPENDIX B
RESOURCE GUIDE

SUGGESTED LIBRARY BOOKS

Structure of Matter by Mark Galan in the *Understanding Science and Nature* series from Time-Life Books – Lots of real-life applications of Chemistry
Inventions and Inventors series from Grolier Educational – Many interesting articles
Molecules by Janice VanCleave – Fun activities
Chemistry for Every Kid by Janice VanCleave – More fun activities
Science Lab in a Supermarket by Bob Friedhoffer – Fun Kitchen Chemistry
Science and the Bible by Donald B. DeYoung – Great biblical applications of scientific ideas
200 Gooey, Slippery, Slimy, Weird & Fun Experiments by Janice VanCleave – More fun activities

SUGGESTED VIDEOS

Newton's Workshop by Moody Institute – Excellent Christian science series, several titles to choose from.
Chemicals to Living Cell: Fantasy or Science (DVD) by Dr. Jonathan Sarfati – The laws of real chemistry show why "goo-to-you" evolution is impossible, available from *Answers in Genesis* (www.AnswersBookstore.com)

SCIENCE SUPPLY RESOURCES

R and D Educational Center
970-686-5744
www.rdeducation.com

Answers in Genesis
800-350-3232
www.AnswersInGenesis.org

Creation Science Resources

Creation Facts of Life by Gary Parker – good explanation of the evidence for creation
The Young Earth by John D. Morris Ph.D – evidence for a young earth
The Answers Book by Ken Ham – answers the most common creation/evolution questions

FIELD TRIP IDEAS

Visit a greenhouse or hydroponics operation to see the use of chemicals with plants.
Tour a battery store to learn about different types of batteries.
Visit a film processing plant to learn about chemicals in film processing.
Visit a pharmacy.
Tour an injection molding plant to learn more about plastics.
Visit a farm to learn about the use of chemicals in farming.

Appendix C

Master Supply List

Supplies needed	Lesson
Vinegar	1, 17, 20, 22
Baking soda	1, 17, 23
Flashlight with battery	6
Copper wire	6
Electrical or duct tape	6, 33
Candle	9, 10, 17
Matches	9, 10, 17
Dry ice	10
Colored mini-marshmallows	11, 12, 13
Toothpicks	11, 12, 13
White glue	11, 12, 13, 32, 34
Silver polish/tarnish remover	14
Epsom salt	15
Polymer clay (Femo, Sculpey, etc.)	16
Modeling clay	17
Jar with lid	17, 20, 29
Hydrogen peroxide	19
Lemon juice	19, 22, 24
Steel wool without soap	20
Thermometer	20
Red/purple cabbage	21
Lemon lime soda pop	22
Ammonia	23
Anti-acid tablets or liquid	23, 24
Toothpaste	23
Swabs	24
2 identical plants – mint plants work well	27
Plant food	27
Garlic powder	28
Ginger ale	28
Rubbing alcohol	29
Whole cloves	29
Balloon	30, 33
Rubber band	30
Glitter	32
Soda straw	33
String	33
Disposable baby diaper	34
Liquid Starch	34
Plastic zipper bags	34

Most art and other supplies should be readily available in most homes.

Appendix D

List of Reproducible Pages

Permission is granted to reproduce the pages listed below for single classroom use.

INDEX

WORKS CITED

Scientists: The Lives and Works of 150 Scientists. Ed. Peggy Saari and Stephen Allison. n.p.: U.X.L An Imprint of Gale, 1996.

Solids, Liquids, and Gases. Ed. Ontario Science Center. Toronto: Kids Can Press, 1998.

"Alexander Fleming." *http://www.pbs.org/wgbh/aso/databank/entries/bmflem.html.* 2004.

Biddle, Verne. *Chemistry Precision and Design.* Pensacola: A Beka Book Ministry, 1986.

Brice, Raphaelle. *From Oil to Plastic.* New York: Young Discovery Library, 1985.

"Charles Goodyear and the Strange Story of Rubber." *Reader's Digest.* Pleasantville, N.Y.: January 1958.

"Charles Martin Hall." *http://www.geocities.com/bioelectrochemistry/hall.htm.* November 2004. "Charles Martin Hall and the Electrolytic Process for Refining Aluminum."

http://www.oberlin.edu/chem/history/cmh/cmharticle.html. 2004. "Charles Martin Hall. "*http://www.corrosion-doctors.org/Biographies/HallBio.htm.* 2004.

Chisholm, Jane, and Mary Johnson. *Introduction to Chemistry.* London: Usborne Publishing, 1983.

Cobb, Vicki. *Chemically Active Experiments You Can Do at Home.* New York: J.B. Lippincott, 1985.

Cooper, Christopher. *Matter.* New York: Dorling Kindersley, 1992.

"Development of the Periodic Table." *http://mooni.fccj.org/~ethall/period/period.htm.* 2004.

"Diapers, the Inside Story." *http://www.chemistry.org/portal/a/c/s/1/wondernetdisplay.html?DOC=wondernet\activities\polymers\diapers.html.* 2004.

Dineen, Jacqueline. *Plastics.* Hillside: Enslow Publishers Inc., 1988.

Dunsheath, Percy. *Giants of Electricity.* New York: Thomas Y. Crowell Co., 1967.

"Farming , Food and Biotechnology." *Inventions and Inventors.* 2000.

Galan, Mark. *Structure of Matter - Understanding Science and Nature.* Alexandria: Time-Life Books, 1992.

"Historical Development of the Periodic Table." *http://members.tripod.com/~EppE/historyp.htm.* 2004.

"How and Why Science in the Water." *World Book.* 1998.

Hughey, Pat. *Scavengers and Decomposers: The Cleanup Crew.* New York: Atheneum, 1984.

Jenkins, John E., and George Mulfinger, Jr. *Basic Science for Christian Schools.* Greenville: Bob Jones University Press, 1983.

Julicher, Kathleen. *Experiences in Chemistry.* Baytown: Castle Heights Press, 1997.

Kuklin, Susan. *Fireworks: the Science, the Art, and the Magic.* New York: Hyperion Books for Children, 1996.

"Marie Curie." *http://www.france.diplomatie.fr/label_france/ENGLISH/SCIENCES/CURIE/marie.html.* 2004.

"Medicine and Health." *Inventions and Inventors.* 2000.

Morris, John D., Ph.D. *The Young Earth.* Colorado Springs: Master Books, 1992.

Newmark, Ann. *Chemistry.* New York: Dorling Kindersley, 1993.

"Nitrogon." www.epa.gov/maia/html/nitrogen.html. 2004.

Parker, Gary. *Creation Facts of Life.* Colorado Springs: Master Books, 1994.

Parker, Steve. *Look at Your Body - Digestion.* Brookfield: Copper Beech books, 1996.

Pinkerton, J.C. "Alexander Fleming and the Discovery of Penicillin." http://nh.essortment.com/alexanderflemin_rmkm.htm.:PageWise, Inc. June 2004.

Richards, Jon. *Chemicals and Reactions.* Brookfield: Copper Beech books, 2000.

"Silly Putty." *www.chem.umn.edu/outreach/Sillyputty.html.* 2004.

Steele, DeWitt. *Observing God's World.* Pensacola: A Beka Books Publishers, 1978.

Student Activities in Basic Science for Christian Schools. Greenville: Bob Jones University Press, 1994.

Thomas, Peggy. *Medicines from Nature.* New York: Twenty-First Century Books, 1997.

VanCleave, Janice. *Chemistry for Every Kid.* New York: John Wiley and Sons, Inc., 1989.

VanCleave, Janice. *Molecules.* New York: John Wiley and Sons, Inc., 1993.

"Vulcanized Rubber." *http://inventors.about.com/library/inventors/blrubber.htm.* 2004.

"WebElements TM Periodic Table (professional edition)." *http://www.webelements.com/index.html.* 2004.